FULL CIRCLE

PARIS
FRANCE

FULL CIRCLE

PANORAMAS BY KENNETH SNELSON

KYOTO
JAPAN

Champs Elysées with l'Arc de Triomphe, 1985

ESSAY BY LAURANCE WIEDER

AFTERWORD BY KENNETH SNELSON

APERTURE

MUSIC BOX
LAURANCE WIEDER

According to an eyewitness, John Wayne walked by falling forward on one foot, and catching himself with the other. In *Relativity,* a book he wrote for laymen, Albert Einstein characterized gravity as the curved earth rolling out to meet the falling object, the falling foot.

    The panoramas photographed over the past decade by Kenneth Snelson subvert the draughtsman's habits: of perspective, of coordinate locations, of projected mental maps. These unorthodox transcriptions of urban monuments, of tourist sights, in Europe and Japan, espouse the enigma of space and its parent time. They measure the cost in optical and mental labor of settling down in a world of grids and intersections, of blocks and regresses and linear mazes. Snelson, whose sculpture explores the ability of elementary structures to extend into space, whose models and computer art propose working and material imitations of hollow spheres of energy (the atom as described by contemporary physics), and whose stereo views shuffle temporal and optical perspective, employs the panoramic camera to depict a photographic alternative to the properties of line, plane, and solid as described in Euclid's *Elements*.

    The artist first experimented with 360-degree images using the Widelux, a camera that records the full panorama in 120-degree increments. The film rests on a curved backing; when the shutter clicks, lens and slitted aperture sweep past the film. The camera is then rotated 120 degrees on its tripod, to expose the adjacent third of the visionary field. A third position fulfills the circle. Snelson usually makes multiple exposures at each of the three camera positions, and assembles the panorama from prints, matching edges among the various exposures. The left-middle-right sequence reflects the compatability of the prints to panoramic marriage, rather than the order in which the photographs were shot. Widelux pictures, such as *Paris Metro, Woman in Red* (page 39), taken in 1975, account for events within a 360-degree neighborhood and even show the curvature of space, but they remain triptychs, rather than seamless renderings of encircling events.

    In the early 1980s, Snelson made a number of monumental black-and-white photographs of such New York City landmarks as Times Square and Brooklyn Bridge using a turn-of-the-century Cirkut camera adapted for his purposes. The Cirkut prints have the presence of stonecarvings: made from a negative sixteen inches high and nearly ten feet long, they are more like architectural elements than photographs. But the size and weight of the camera, the special-order film and paper, and the custom darkroom Snelson had to design and build to process and reproduce his images, added up to a lot of trouble and effort just to take and show a photograph. To explore non-Euclidean sights in foreign cities, the artist needed a machine that didn't require him to be porter, laboratory technician and special-order clerk as well as photographer.

    The panoramic photographs reproduced in this book were made with a Hulcherama camera. Small enough to transport, and using stock color film, it operates on the same principle as the Cirkut camera. A motor rotates the camera counterclockwise on its tripod axis through an arc of as many degrees, or as many full turns, as the photographer desires. Gears advance the film in time with the sweep of the lens. Each pan/exposure is a seamless unit. The scroll-like prints can be read as narratives, from right to left as in Japanese or Hebrew. Where Widelux panoramas are mosaic assemblages with sequence but no starting or stopping place, these panoramas have a beginning and an end. Where the triptychs consist of three photographic segments, three adjacent investigations outside of time, the continuous panorama records duration in a single scan that can't be read in one glance. Widelux pictures analyze a full-circle view. Seamless panoramas synthesize a new vision of the old world.

Normally, looking down the avenue, the way recedes toward a vanishing point where parallel curbs meet. At intersections, streets approach each other at right angles, cross and recede. Stand at the corner and the lines of intersection run straight through you. The grid system implies that phenomena can touch us, and that we, by the same token, can enter the world. Objectifying position means seeing oneself from above, on a map, in coordinate relationship to established landmarks. In the panorama, intersections of road and road, self and scene, do not occur. Instead, objects swerve up and veer away, like a speedboat making a power turn. The world which encloses the viewer, and may be reconstituted by mating the ends of the panorama and placing one's head inside the cylinder, can never be touched, cannot be grasped.

The square in front of the Basilica of San Marco, in Venice, ranks with the gondola as an emblem of the city. In the eighteenth century, Johann Wolfgang Goethe's father gave the child a toy gondola, black wood with metal prow ornament and carpeted cockpit, identical to the model my father brought me when I was eight. In his *Italian Journey*, the forty-year-old Goethe recalled his childhood treasure, and marveled at its fidelity to the full-size vessel. In *Baedeker's* map, as in Gentile Bellini's 1496 painting *Procession in Piazza San Marco*,[1] the Basilica stands at the east end of an L-shaped plaza, anchored to the south by the Campanile. The long side of the L, the "square," is defined by the (old) Procuratie Vecchie to the north, and the sixteenth-century Nuove Procuratie on the south. The Museo Correr borders the narrower west end of the square, which is actually a trapezoid. The geometry and perspective of the piazza would be skewed under any circumstances, overwhelmed by the splendor of the Basilica.

The panoramic photograph, *Piazza S. Marco, Venice* (page 43), however, reorders that magnificence. In a picture taken as the sun rose behind the cathedral, the camera scanned counterclockwise from west (the museum with its IMPRESSIONISTI banner) to south (the Procuratie Nuove), past the Campanile and San Marco itself in the east, the Procuratie Vecchie in the north, to finish again in the west. Snelson set up closer to the Vecchie on the north, doubtless so the bell tower would not obscure the cathedral, and far enough west to include most of the Campanile's height in the photograph. While it is relatively simple to deduce the vantage point in this picture, the artist himself cannot always work out just where he stood. Nor can he always locate where objects pictured in the panorama stand in the usual geography of experience, or depiction. Although reversing the process of making these photographs may be a way to take bearings, to assume a posture toward these unusual transcriptions of famous places, reconstructing deconstructed space only leads from the uncanny back to the iconic.

Returning to the *Piazza*, the panoramic rearrangement of space has redirected visual emphasis, if not moral order. Looking east down the upsilon-shaped funnel of the square, the paving stones present a pattern of intersecting fan shapes, fans opening toward the bottom of the picture. The white floor-plan designs that form aprons parallel to the old and new

Procuratie now curve like lips. The Campanile, a clock and bell tower where sixteenth-century Sodomites were suspended in small cages and fed on bread and water for extended periods, dwarfs the apparently distant cathedral. Where the old administrative buildings and the museum exhibit bow in the panoramic portrait, in tune with the paving stones, the eponymous historic, touristic, not to mention fideist focus of the site dwindles, and does not bend. At the print's center, a wooden construction shed obscures the arches to the north of the Basilica's main entrance. Over the main doors, where the four bronze horses taken from the hippodrome in Constantinople were displayed from the mid-thirteenth century until 1979, stands a plywood enclosure. At the center of the photograph, the phantom image of a passerby strikes a transparent pose.

Kenneth Snelson is interested in European cities as monuments and as stages for monumental works. Times Square enjoys no less fame than The Louvre and is a watchword to boot, but it is only a site, an idea, an intersection, like a place name in the desert. A photograph of the crossroads of the world records only one neon moment, panorama notwithstanding. Venice, Siena, Assisi, Rome, and Paris, by contrast, display long passages of history in uncovered stalls. In these cities, the fleeting or compliant confronts the lasting or intransigent, the externalized passions of the long-dead compete with the pretensions of the living.

In *Le Louvre* (page 25), the camera scans 800 years of French history in one revolution of the lens. Ornamental boxwood planted in the shape of fleurs-de-lys, emblem of the Bourbon kings of France (1589–1830), fills the foreground of the photograph. From this bed (actually a green island in the Place du Carrousel), even nature is an aspect of artifice, and the only straight line is a circle. The Capetian King Phillippe Auguste (reigned 1180–1223) originally built a fortress at this site on the Seine to defend his newly walled city of Paris. The panoramic photograph of this palace constructed piecemeal on the site of a fortress built by Phillippe Auguste starts (right to left) in the century of the two French Empires, with additions erected by emperors Napoleon I (1804–14) and Napoleon III (1851–73). These terminate in Louis XIV's (1643–1715) Pavillon de Marsan (here under repair, and hooded by a construction envelope). Trees in the Tuileries Garden occupy the space between the Marsan and a triumphal arch erected between 1806–08 to celebrate Napoleonic victories in 1805; until 1815, the arch displayed the four bronze horses from the basilica of Saint Marks, Venice, liberated by Napoleon I. Continuing to the left, the print shows: Henri IV's (1589–1610) Pavillon de Flore (with Second Empire additions); the Galerie du Bord de l'Eau, built by Catherine de Medici (1547–60) and largely obscured by Napoleon III's additions flanking the Cour Napoleon III; a graffitied barricade that hides construction of I.M. Pei's glass pyramid, commissioned by François Mitterrand of the Fifth Republic (1981–89). Also blocked by the construction fence are a Louis XIV addition to Catherine de Medici's addition; the "Old Louvre" begun in 1546 under François I (1515–47); and the aptly named Pavillon de l'Horloge, a contribution from Louis XIII (1610–43). The last quarter of this print depicts the balance of the Napoleonic structures shown at the start. The revolution ends where it began, at the Sun King's Pavillon de Marsan. The panoramic camera's customary wit, which presents adjacent spaces as plane neighbors, has been anticipated by the Louvre, which juxtaposes 450 years of diverse yet absolute self-assertion as wings of a single palace. Snelson's panorama of the entire facade bounding the Napoleonic Court realigns centuries of twisting political intrigue and treachery, lays them out like an optical Haussmann plotting boulevards through the alleys of old Paris. The leveling if not flattening power of the panoramic print puts deceit and violence as monumentalized in the great museum's architecture in or on the same plane as graffiti, new construction, restoration, crowds, a sports car, a man and a dog in a crosswalk. The sweep of this inclusive plane, and its chromatic gaiety, suggest a nineteenth-century color lithograph, or political cartoon. The barricade and the lawn at center of the print, shaped like wedges from a large pie, would then no doubt be just desserts. To the victor. Time is a great egalitarian.

Another Paris photograph, *Pont Neuf with Ile de la Cité* (page 17), was taken halfway across the bridge linking the banks of the Seine with the western tip of the river island. The camera was set up in one of the stone coves that surmounts each bridge pier. A pair of iron streetlamps flanks each cove. The river flows under the bridge and west, toward the Louvre, its rooftops just visible about three-quarters or 270 degrees to the left. Because the tripod has raised the camera above the stone balustrade, the outermost arc of the cove lies outside the picture.

Panoramas cannot be read in a glance. This raises questions not only about camera vantage, but also about the reader's point of view. Mathematically speaking, "straight ahead" in these pictures lies at every point along the length of the photographic print. The roughly twenty-one inches of panorama exceeds the full circle of 360 degrees by anywhere from ten to twenty degrees. This overlap or repetition "frames" the scene naturally, and punctuates the revolution. Allowing 20 inches = 360 degrees, each inch of print represents 18 degrees of rotation. If my eye settles between the lampposts on Bridge Nine, that point becomes the front. Ten inches to the left, the print shows what is located directly behind me, were I standing at the site of the photograph. Events and objects at right angles to my line of sight, and so presumably at the limit of my peripheral vision, are recorded in the region five inches to either side of the front of the picture. In *Pont Neuf*, the river bank which breaks at either end of the print is the South (or Left) bank. The river flowing toward the left and the Louvre, so smoothly that it intensifies the marbled overcast it mirrors, comes from upstream straight in front of me, and passes under the bridge and my feet. Were it not for the absent rail on the stone embrasure, I would be in the water, excluded from the scene completely. As it is, the phantom cyclist beside the near-right streetlamp shows his embodied back ninety degrees later to the left, apparently launched into visibility by the sling-shaped bridge.

The panoramic camera has the uncanny capacity for depicting befuddlement and orthodoxy with a comic beauty more often found in Mozart's operas than in photography. The requirements of logic and consistency dominate the narrative arts, and frustrate the representation of the incongruous, the superfluous, the contradictory and arbitrary. But all bets are off in Librettoland. Musical space, like musical reasoning, operates by different rules. This alternative structure reveals itself in the simple scale.[2] The eight notes of the octave, say from C to C, are heard as rising or falling, leaving and returning, hence the expression ascending or descending scales. Symbolically, the quavers ascend the rungs of the staff, visually reinforcing what the ear already knows. Intellectually, the journey from C to C is recognized as circular, an eternal recurrence perhaps like those journeys that return a changed traveler to the place he first set out, or the new new moon.

The scientist measuring scales on the oscilloscope finds no support for the evidence of his ears. The tones, which are heard as steps on a spiral staircase, register only as a circle on the screen of the physicist's instrument. Overtones, undertones, color, intonation: none of the properties of heard melodies exist in that measured world. Plotted against time, the circle graphed on the printout is a sine wave.

Musical space is coextensive with visual space, but different. Although visual, panoramic space exhibits many of the properties of musical space. It represents straight lines as arcs of a great circle; the horizon, and other concentric circles, become straight lines. Cities, built on grids, open up: streets do not intersect, rather each runs parallel to the others; enclosed squares become cement scallops, courtyards appear as walls. Music and the panorama share other qualities, such as periodicity and temporality, but these, as T.S. Eliot said of meaning in poetry, are just the bit of meat the burglar throws to the house dog. Like music, the real panorama is interior. Our pair of eyes confront no more than one-third of the visible scene in any glance, the visible regarded as the surface of the material, a convex "out there." The panoramic camera transcribes the visible, but as seen from the center of a transparent cylinder—a surface that encloses and is viewed from within. This interiority panoramas share with music. Again, the inner works of a music box realize a melody recorded (in steel teeth) on the surface of a revolving drum, performed or unrolled in time, when the spring is wound, and the lid opened. In both media, the resonances are psychological. The startling panoramic photograph calls not the maker nor the work but the viewer into question, playing the impulse to see and know everything against the improbable shape of that partially gratified appetite. Is there a music that I cannot hear?

Earlier in this century, Russian composer and mystic Aleksandr Scriabin was building a piano that would play colors and music, when death claimed him. His fellow countryman, amateur cellist and pioneer nonrepresentational artist Wassilly Kandinsky, devoted the opening pages of his book *Point and Line to Plane* to a visual representation of the first bars of Beethoven's *Fifth Symphony*. The Swiss painter Paul Klee supported himself for years as second violist in the Basel orchestra; in the first volume of his notebooks, *The Thinking Eye,* Klee extensively analyzes the musical aspects of the visual. Composers Erik Satie and Arnold Schoenberg were also active visual artists. Schoenberg's student Anton Webern employed what he called "Klangfarbe" (sound colors) in his rigorous compositions.

For Klee, Kandinsky, and Schoenberg, the materials of art and music provided a way into the world, the single source of all knowledge. The separate arts approach or report the same truth through different organs, the form of that intelligence also determined by the inherent nature of the art material. The individual artist testifies to the structure and operation of the external (what Paul Klee called "the nature of nature") with the same authority as the scientist, whose presence as observer also shapes or alters the data recorded by his experiments.

In spirit, Snelson's art resembles Webern's music. Webern was no painter, and Snelson is not a composer or instrumentalist. However, both artists have developed idioms that refer to a world independent of the individual's psychic journey. Their works arise out of their materials, and take form according to, or perhaps articulate, objective principles. A Snelson sculpture or panorama refers to the external world, not to a chapter from the artist's autobiography. The autonomous creation is no doubt cousin to the *perpetuum mobile* and the *golem,* but it need not be the creation of a mad scientist or a rabbi. In Snelson's work, as in Webern's, purity of expression and abhorrence of bombast characterize artistic languages that are certainly beautiful, and fiercely modest, though not sweet, confessional, or vainglorious.

If the music of the Louvre and the Piazza of San Marco is reorchestrated symphony, then the photograph *Inner court, Siena* (page 75) is a chamber duet. Light and darkness interplay with an authority that transcends genre, setting, and locale. I understand that this is a panorama, that the sickle of sunlight on the courtyard floor is actually a narrow rectangle, that the dark hall giving out on the dazzling square leads directly to the stairs. I prefer to read this picture as a portrait of what is known, and how. The window, half-open door, and crescent of sunshine appear to be the eye, nose, and smile of a Cheshire cat, seen from inside its skull. The smile's lower lip is part of the S-curve dividing the region of light from that dominated by darkness. Wall plaques, a low doorway on the far right nearly lost in the gloom, the bulletin board with its small lamp highlighting some posted notice, and the pillar supporting the vaulted entry to the stairs furnish the dark side of the interior. On the left, a small stone lion bathed in sunlight sits atop the newel post like the bust of some bewigged Enlightenment philosopher. His domain comprehends the bannister of a stairway that appears to lead nowhere; a wooden door with arched transom; another, smaller door (possibly the same as the door of darkness on the other side of the print); and plaques as indecipherable in daylight as they are in obscurity. A Trinity of presences, doubtless reflections beamed down in front of the door, hover like weird sisters or robed monks. Where the panoramas of public spaces yield a narrative, critique, or theatrical commentary latent in the details, this image detaches from the circumstances of its inscription and firmly plays both parts in a presto of knowledge and uncertainty. As the work of a machine, it's difficult to call this photograph lyrical or personal, but it does suggest the intimacy of some truth held in common that, were there words for it, might be confessed.

Japanese cities do not last like those built around the Mediterranean Sea. The emperors' capitals were made of wood and paper. As the prizes of war, as the victims of fire, flood, and earthquake, as objects of ambition, abandonment, and neglect, few structures survived even a century, much less the 1500 years recorded in Japanese histories. Temples and monasteries fared somewhat better, but the monks' penchant for combat and politics usually doomed their compounds when their worldly order fell from power's grace. Most notable of the fighting priests were the monks of Mt. Hiei, a group so influential that for centuries it retained virtual veto over affairs of state, and so troublesome that Oda Nobunaga was compelled to level the place in 1571 as part of his successful campaign to end nearly two centuries of civil war.

The Dragon Peace Temple, Ryoan-ji, was first constructed, burned, and rebuilt, during the fifteenth century. The Zen temple's rock garden dates from about 1500, and is traditionally credited to the monk So-ami. Unharmed when the temple burned again in the 1790s, the rock garden stands much as it did 500 years ago, although the rebuilt temple clusters more tightly around the stone yard than in its monastic heyday. "Discovered" in 1930, late enough to be spared domestic upheaval but just in time for the world picture press, the meditation garden was photographed from every imaginable angle. Photos of the place became a spiritual banality, yet efforts to convey the essence of "the mystery" in image and commentary were just so much ink and paper, with little connection to the fifteen boulders half-buried in the white gravel garden.

Monastic retreat from the world of affairs is the historical and literary alternative to a life of care and obligations for the Japanese layman, be he servant or master. Though the break with the world was seldom so clear-cut as the tonsured head might suggest, temple gardens are truly settings for solitary retreat and meditation, rather than leafy clubs where citizens stroll, loll, and chat, such as the museum and hotel gardens Snelson photographed in Paris. Zen meditation might be described as a path to the present, a way to see what is, as distinct from what is thought to be, so that ties to the world can be relinquished. This formulation points not toward enlightenment, whatever that might mean, but toward a kinship with Snelson's panoramic image, *Rock Garden, Ryoan-ji Temple, Kyoto* (page 85).

At the center of this photograph, looking east down the veranda running between the rock garden and the *hojo* (superior's quarters), is a dark recess. The rock garden on the right, and the continuation of the veranda, *hojo*, and a moss garden on the left appear as through cat's eyes. The eyes are defined by the intersecting sine waves graphed as the camera cycled past the veranda roof and floor. The cat's left eye is half-shut; the right watches the rock garden. Except for a cutout at the newer east end, the garden is rectangular. A mud-and-oil wall encloses the south and west bounds. The west wall, on the right here, is 6–8 inches higher at the north, where it meets the building, than it is at the southwest corner, where it joins the long south wall. The trees beyond, now grown to full height after four centuries, were the object of this perspectival manipulation by the garden's designer: the "farther" wall acting as a sill to the "borrowed landscape" would have created the illusion of a deep vista.

In the Sienese courtyard, the heat of the outside world does not pass through the minatory door and window. In this Japanese enclosure light and shadows, inside and outside, balance in a poised, an active, interpenetration. The "pair of eyes" invites an instantaneous reading of the photograph, an eye for an eye as it were, rather than a narration unscrolled from right to left. The panorama has enlarged the gate to the present. The immediate may be no easier to apprehend, but the wider the eye opens, the more it admits of the external. Music in this garden [is] the twanging of a single string.

Ryoan-ji stands on a 127-acre estate established by the powerful Fujiwara family in Heian times. Seven imperial tombs stand on a hill to the north of the temple site. Among them are Uda (reigned 887–97), the first retired emperor to become a Buddhist priest; Ichijo (986–1011), whose brilliant literary court included Sei Shonagon, author of *The Pillow Book,* and Lady Murasaki Shikibu, who wrote *The Tale of Genji;* and Go-Sanjo (1068–72), the only emperor to actually govern from Kyoto during its thousand-plus years as the national capital, from its foundation by the emperor Kammu (781–806) until the seat of power was moved to Tokyo in 1868. Snelson's other panorama, *Ryoan-ji Temple, Kyoto* (page 77), portrays a large temple building and small Buddhist shrine at the southwest corner of the same hill where the rock garden sits. The white gravel path leading from the Heian lake below goes straight uphill. The switchback created by the panoramic camera intensifies the steepness of the ascent, a perspective exaggeration common in both *emaki* (Japanese narrative scrolls) and in Chinese landscape scrolls. The path leading up from the world to the place of Amida Buddha should not appear easy.

The analogy with oriental scrolls feels obligatory, a substitute for entering the spirit of the picture, and indicates just how far away, how foreign, the Japanese photographs lie from my experience. Literature and painting provide the mental tourist with other maps of the unfamiliar. But the great strength of these panoramas is their ability to refresh the tired, restore the overfamiliar sight to an unmanageable objectivity.

Engineer Gustave Eiffel designed and built his tower for the 1889 Paris Exhibition. The Eiffel Tower was scheduled to be removed from its site at the river end of the Champ-de-Mars after twenty years, but its conversion in 1904 to a radio-telegraphy transmitter-receiver saved the icon from the wrecker. This prototype wireless transmission tower (like that at the start of every "RKO Radio Picture") is reproduced inside glass balls that make snowstorms when shaken, as a souvenir pencil sharpener, and as the subject of innumerable travelogues, postcards, newsreels, art and amateur photographs.

Snelson's *River Seine with Eiffel Tower* (page 41), shows the latticework landmark from a point on the North or Right Bank, just west of the Pont de Bir-Hakeim. Though the appearance and disappearance of a pedestrian under the arched pier supporting the Metro tracks tells a little story as the camera pans from right to left, the photograph centers on the 330-meter tower's sway over the Parisian sky. The bronze neighing horse and sword-wielding rider point from somewhere on the far side of the nineteenth century at this border post between Romanticism and heavy industry.

Guide books commend the views of Paris from the three platforms on the tower. I remember my childhood terror watching the stairway turn through the near leg as my parents took me on the elevator to the first platform. I did not believe the concrete and steel platform was not swaying; no coaxing could convince me that I would not be blown from the tower by the zephyr sifting through the girders, and I declined the invitation to go higher.

The plaza at the tower's base, a square projected by the enormous structure overhead, inspired a more manageable unease. In *Bust of Gustave Eiffel with Tower* (page 19), the presence of bystanders testifies to the arresting power of this ceilinged space. Groups stand outside the shadow of the first platform. Individuals and clutches of tourists crossing underneath either pause and stare upwards, or walk slowly enough to fully materialize in the panorama. From the vantage of the fourth leg, or corner, of the tower, the camera scans the open pavement beginning at the gold-leaf bust of Gustave Eiffel. The other legs of the tower appear behind an island of lawn and flowers, condensed by the panoramic perspective into a single three-footed corner. The paving-stone walk in the foreground curves upward at the picture's corners in a toothy Coney Island smile. The grin, taken with the eyes suggested by the pair of arches between the three legs, imparts an anthropomorphic quality to the scene. The engineer Eiffel, gazing slightly upward, and his tower, leering from the print, bring this print to the verge of rhetoric.

Justice demands that this temporary structure which has survived five of its own lifetimes, has seen two World Wars and three Republics, so often the subject of photographs that its has lost its objectivity, should be endowed with an expressive visage by a fellow machine. By showing banality as it could never be seen, yet as it is, the panorama proposes a knowledge that restores some portion of our innocence. Or letting Eden lapse, these photographs make the overfamiliar unfamiliar. Those conventional images of the Eiffel Tower shot every year at every season and every time of day from every imaginable angle make it impossible to see the Eiffel Tower for the first time. They degrade us from mere ignorant children to children who think we know it all beforehand. These panoramas, optically outrageous yet transcriptively faithful, restore the boundary between object and subject, by making the mind struggle to reclaim what it thought it knew.

Kenneth Snelson's panoramic photographs stake out unexplored territory that's easily located on a map. What his camera records impeaches the authority of both the eye and the still photograph as reliable witnesses to the nature and structure of space. For several weeks after I first read and understood Albert Einstein's *Relativity,* I missed steps, walked into doors that I usually opened without thought, and had difficulty discriminating near from far. Although I reoriented, I never fully recovered confidence in my relationship to the physical world. These panoramas induce and explore that same uncertainty. A mechanical response to the "hast thou considered . . ." of Job, they leap over the self-regarding issues of How to go on? How to evolve without catastrophe? How to make it, make it new, make it whole beyond the arbitrary frame, the picaresque, the accidental neighborhood? Instead, they open a frontier and ask Where are we? What is space? How does time pass, inside and out? A lot to ponder, teetering on the rim of a place that just existed as a rumor, leaning forward for a better view, like a scout played by John Wayne would, searching the curved limits of the habitable.

1. Reproduced in Christopher Hibbert, *Venice: The Biography of a City,* W.W. Norton & Co., New York, New York, color plate between pp. 116–117.

2. I first learned about the "mystery of the octave" as summarized here from Victor Zuckerkandl, *Sound and Symbol: Music and the External World,* Bollingen Series XLIV, Princeton University Press, Princeton, New Jersey. Zuckerkandl uses this anomalous discrepancy between psychology and physics as a logical proof of the existence of spirit.

PARIS

River Seine, early morning, 1985

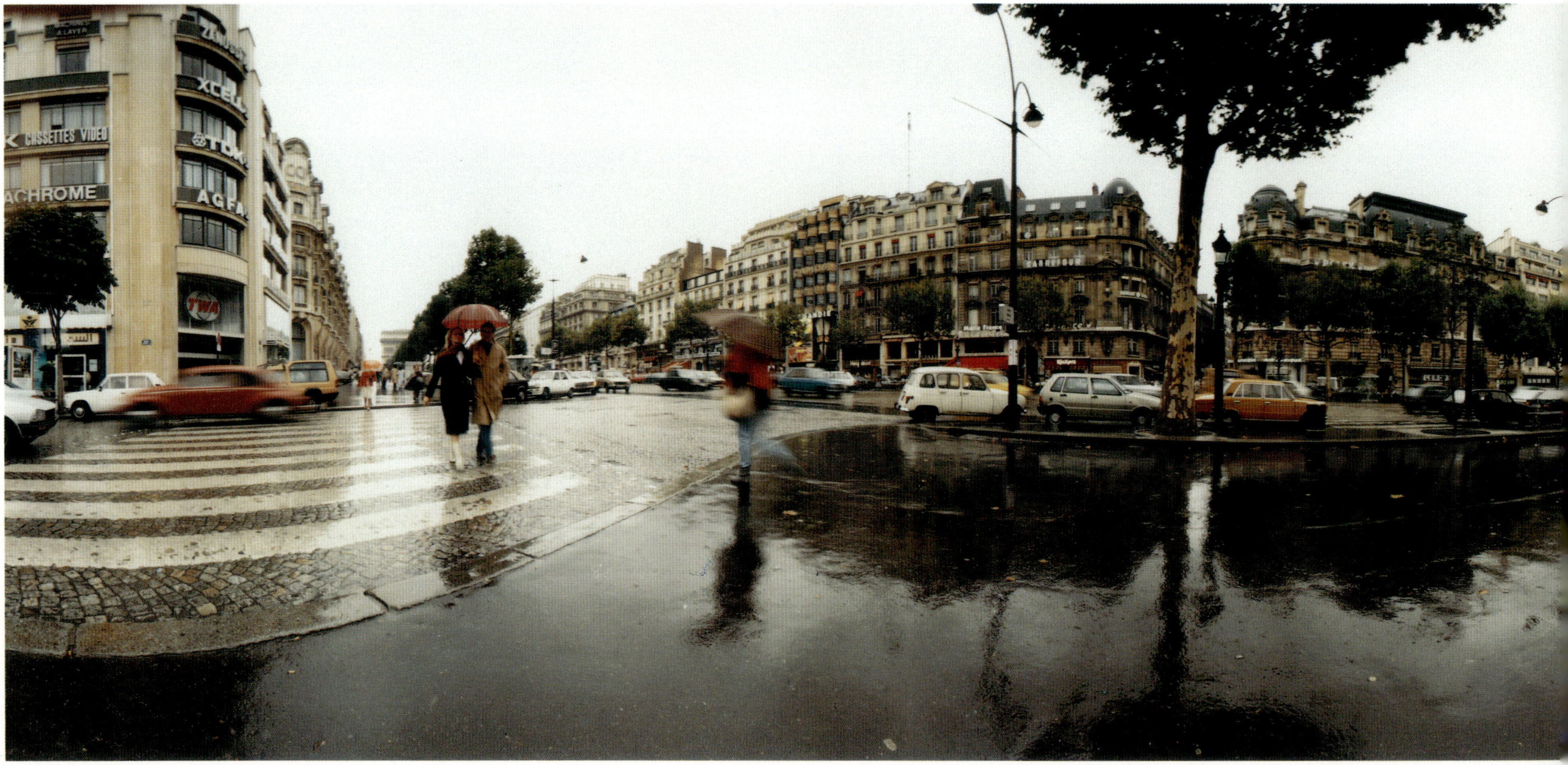

Rain, Champs Elysées, 1985

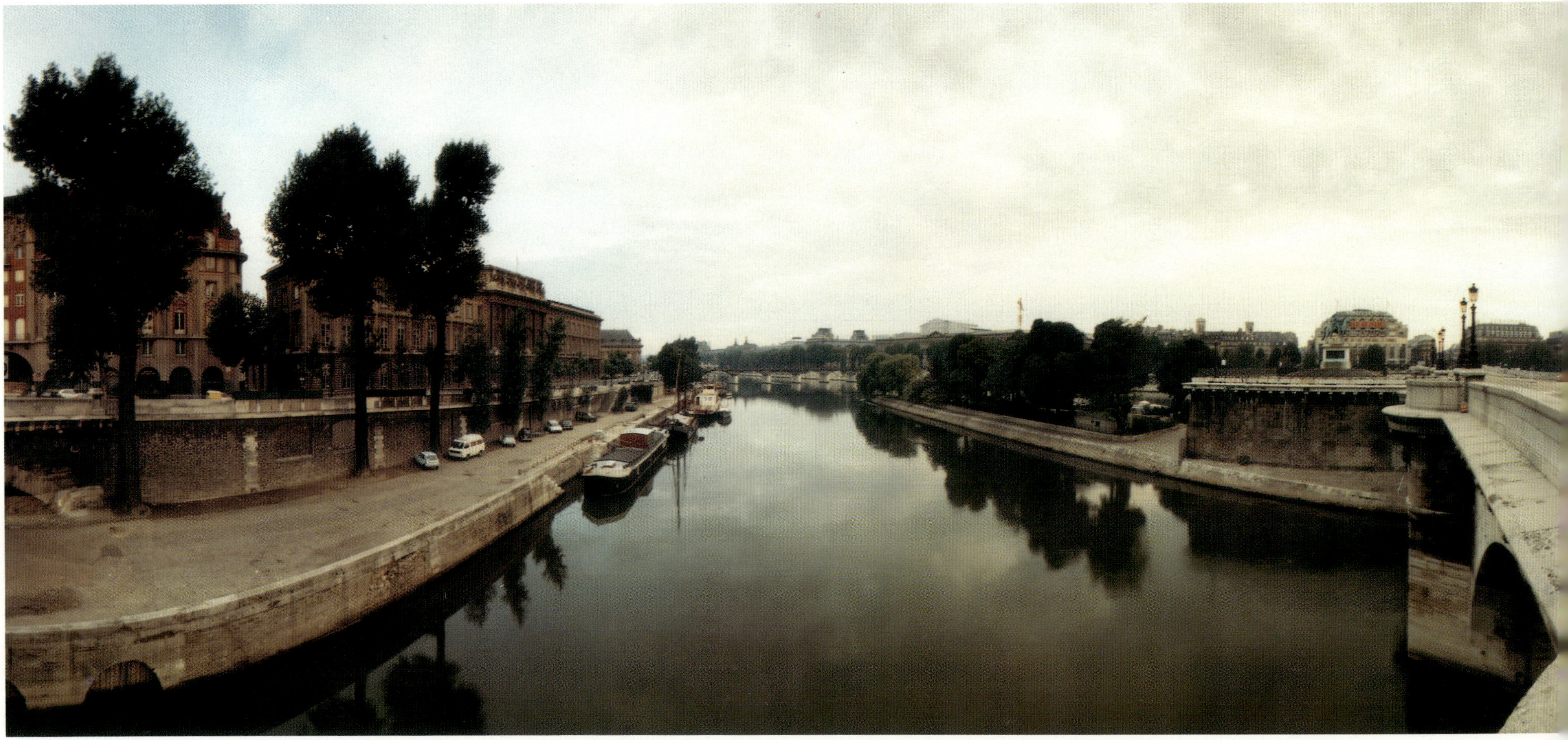

Pont Neuf with Ile de la Cité, 1985

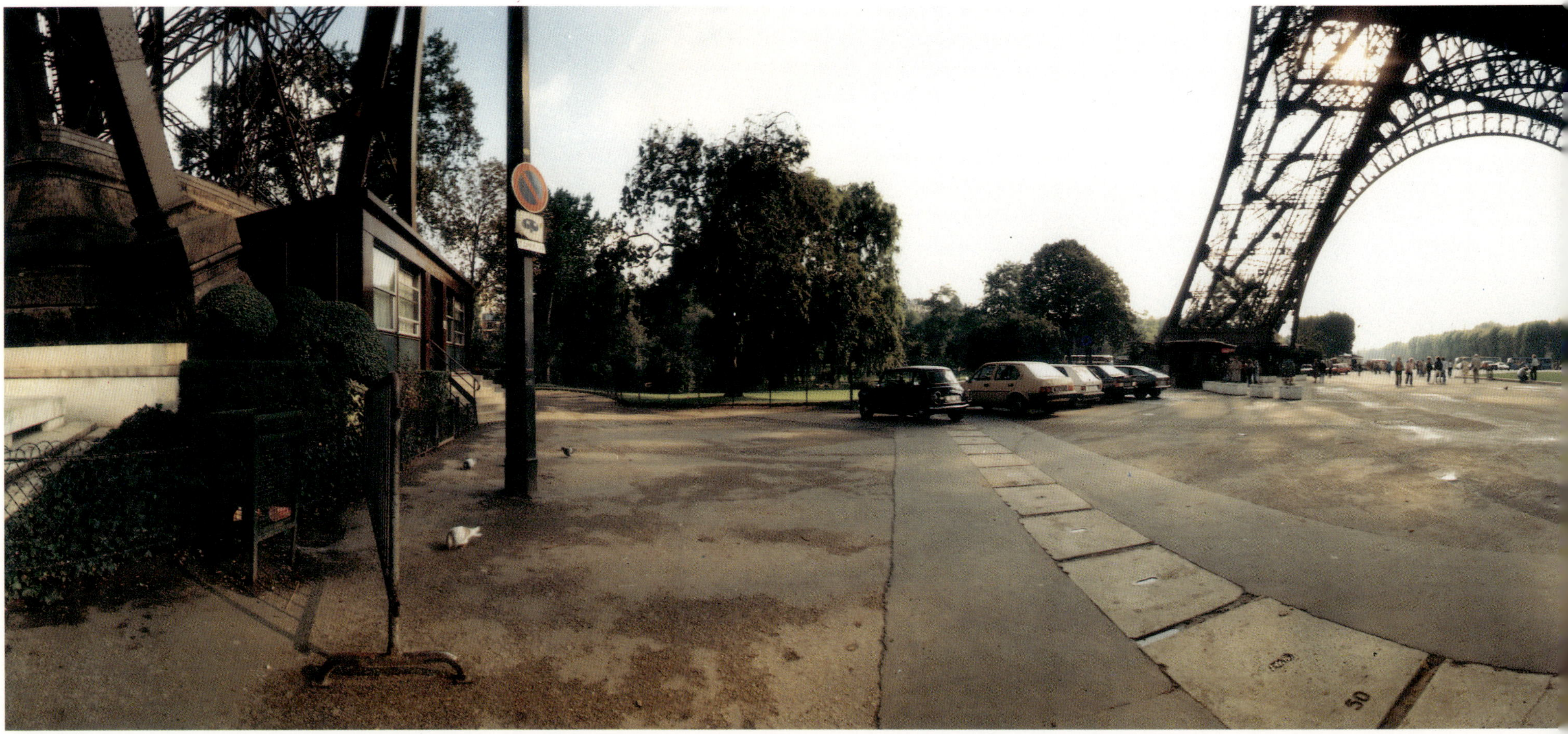

Bust of Gustave Eiffel with Tower, 1985

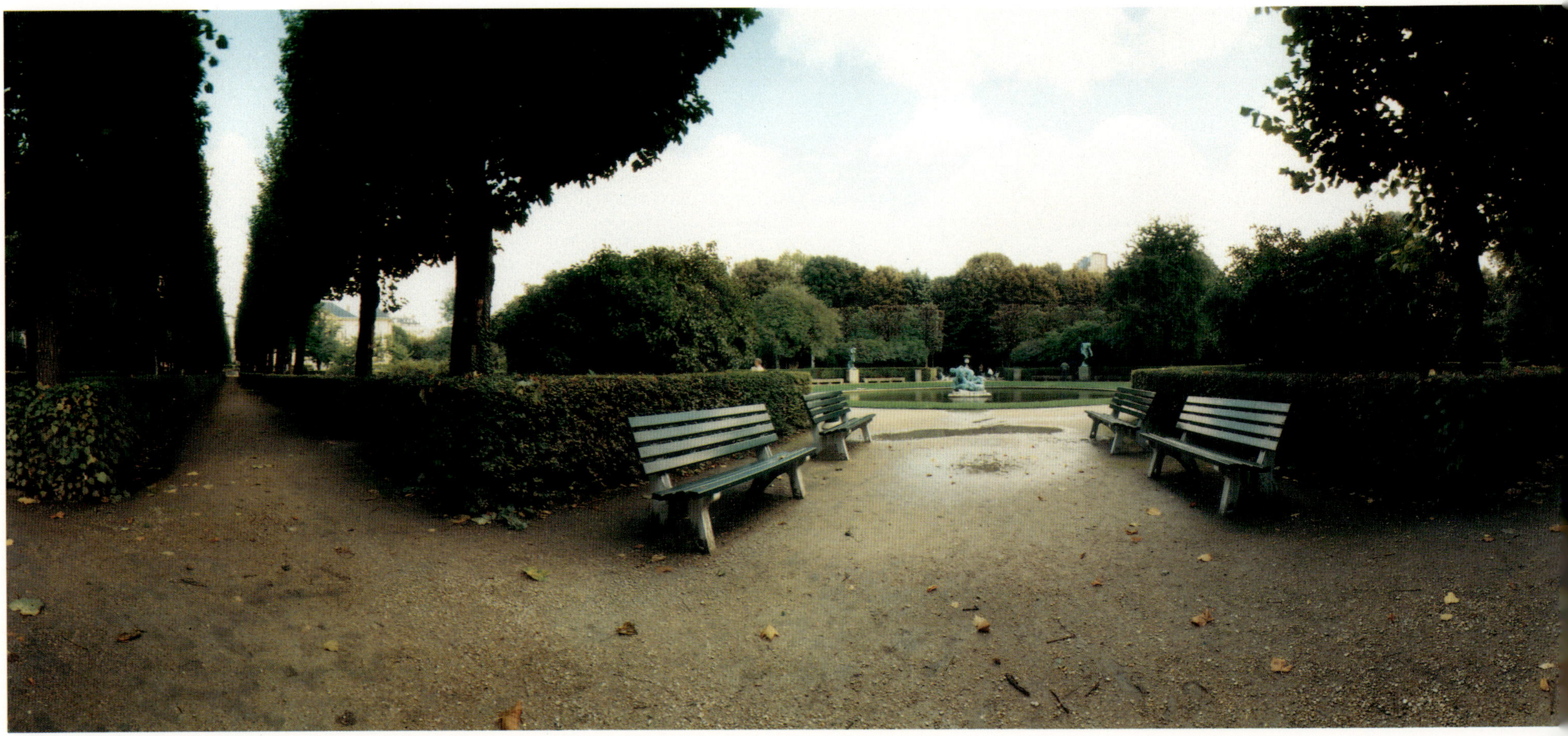

Garden of Musée Rodin, 1985

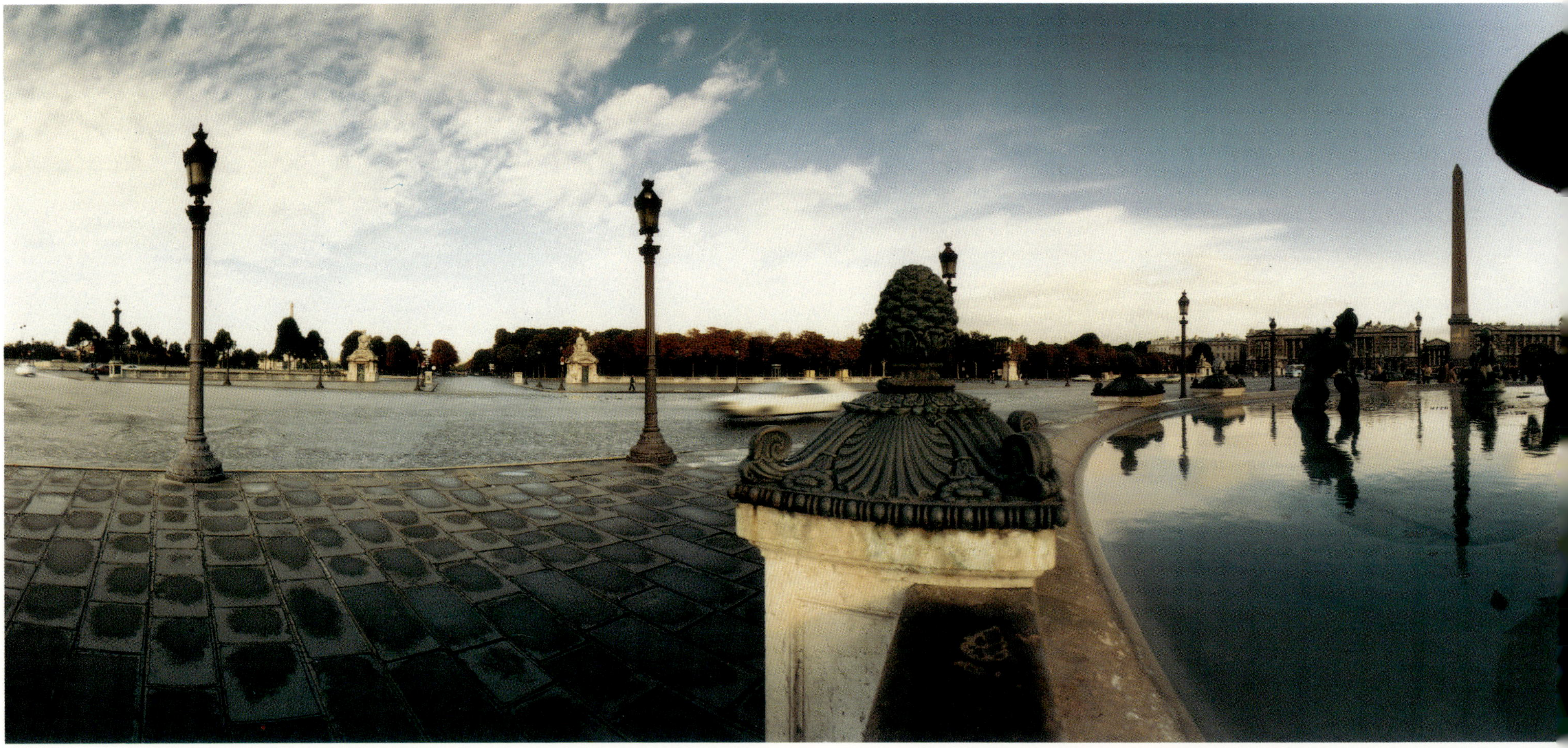

Fountain, Place de la Concorde, 1985

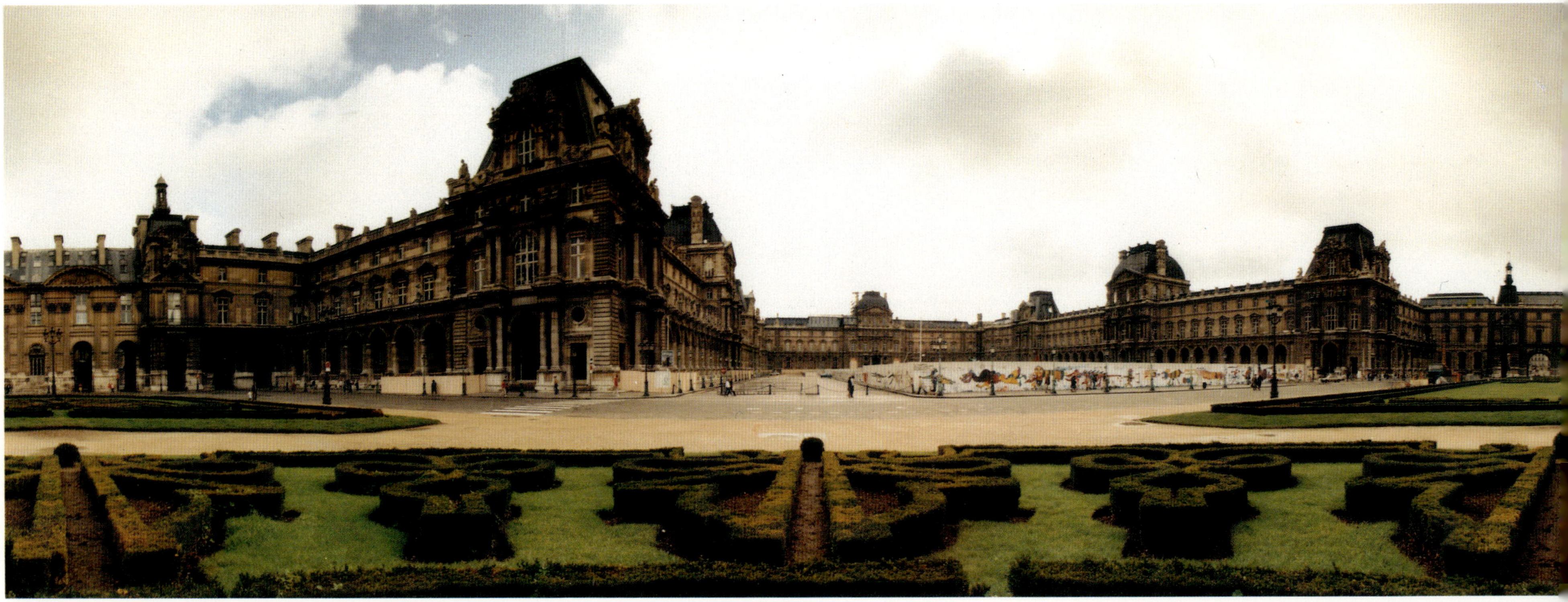

Le Louvre, 1985

PAPETERIE
ACHAT DE CHEVAUX
LE MARIGNY
LE MARIGNY
CAFE-TABAC
LE MARIGNY

Paris street scene with red horse, 1975

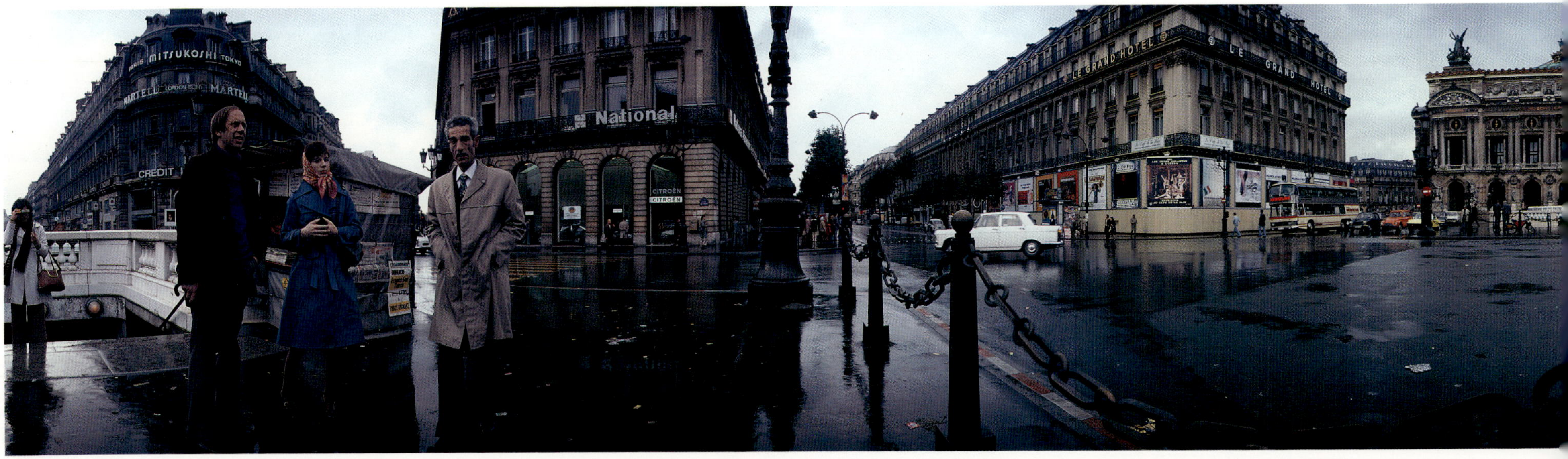
MITSUKOSHI
MARTELL
National
CITROËN
LE GRAND HOTEL

L'Opera, 1975

CINEMA
FRITES
2000
RESTAURANT
PLATS A EMPORTER
RESTAURANT
cinema
LOCATION
VENTE
NOUVEAUTES

Cinema Drugstore, 1985

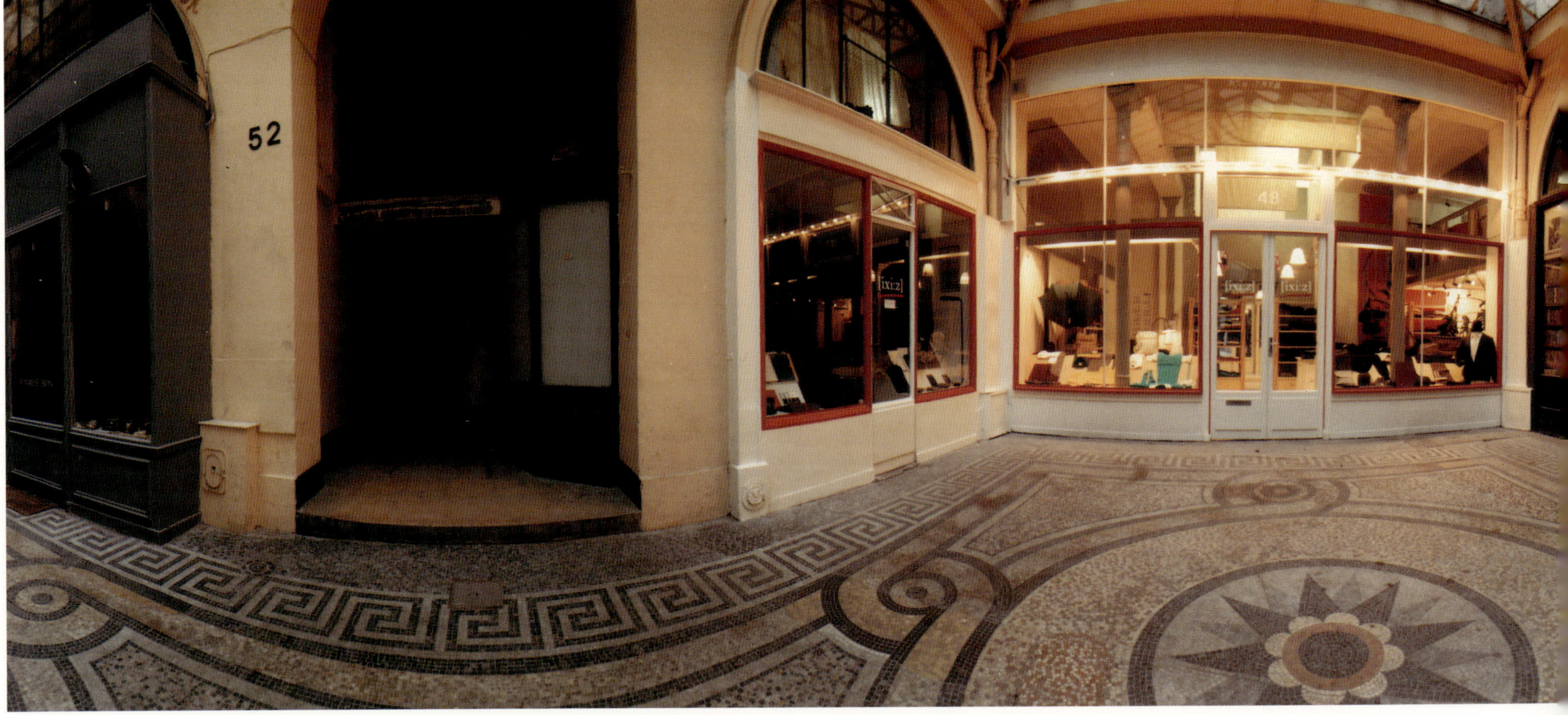
52
48
[ixi:z]

Galeria with clothing store, 1985

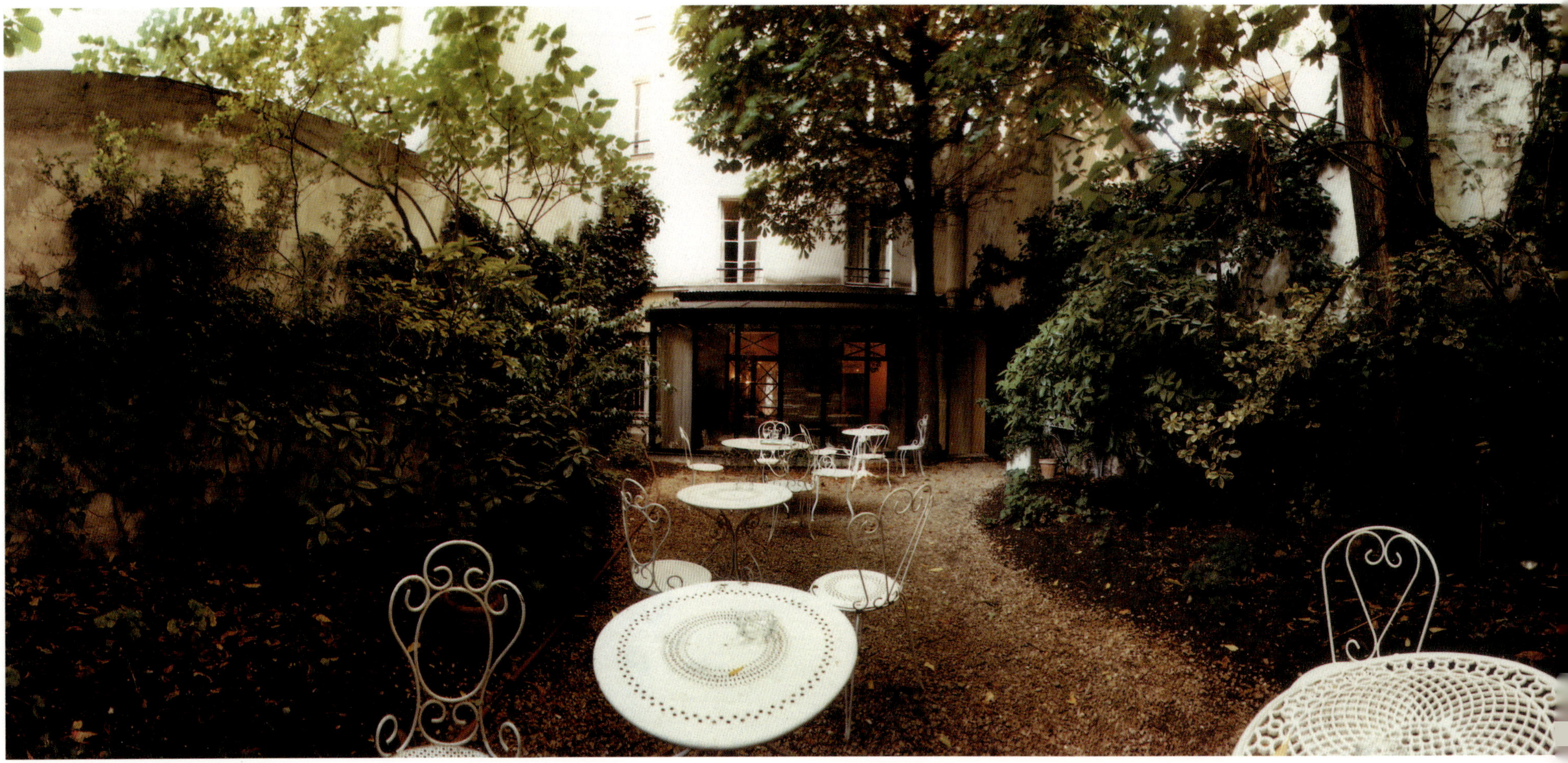

Garden of Hotel des Marroniers, 1985

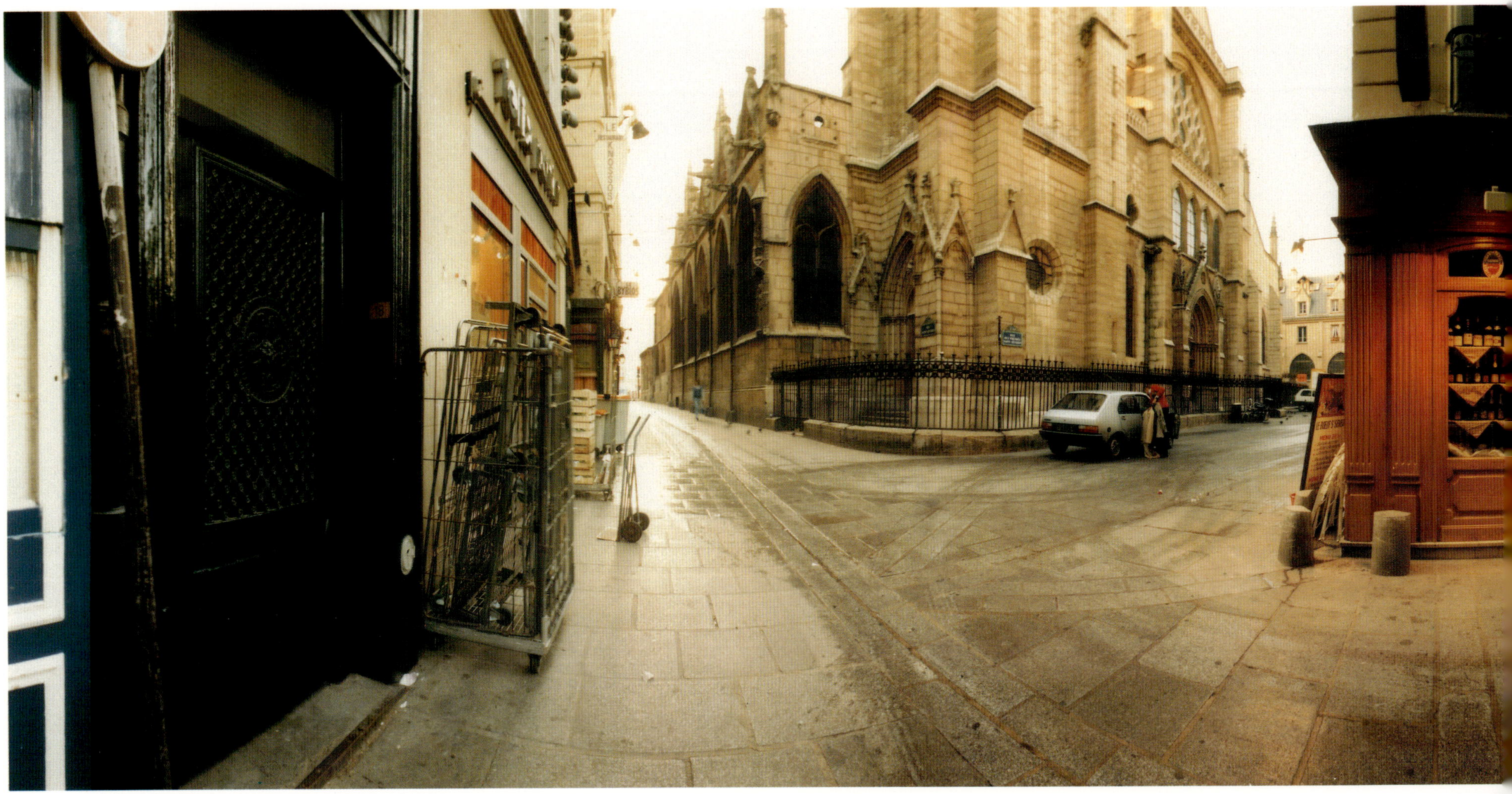

Rue des Pretres St. Severin with Brasserie, 1985

SORTIE
BIR-HAKEIM
GRENELLE
BIR-HAKEIM
GRENELLE
Galfa Club.
Redécouvrez le costume.
Galeries Lafayette

Paris Metro, woman in red, 1975

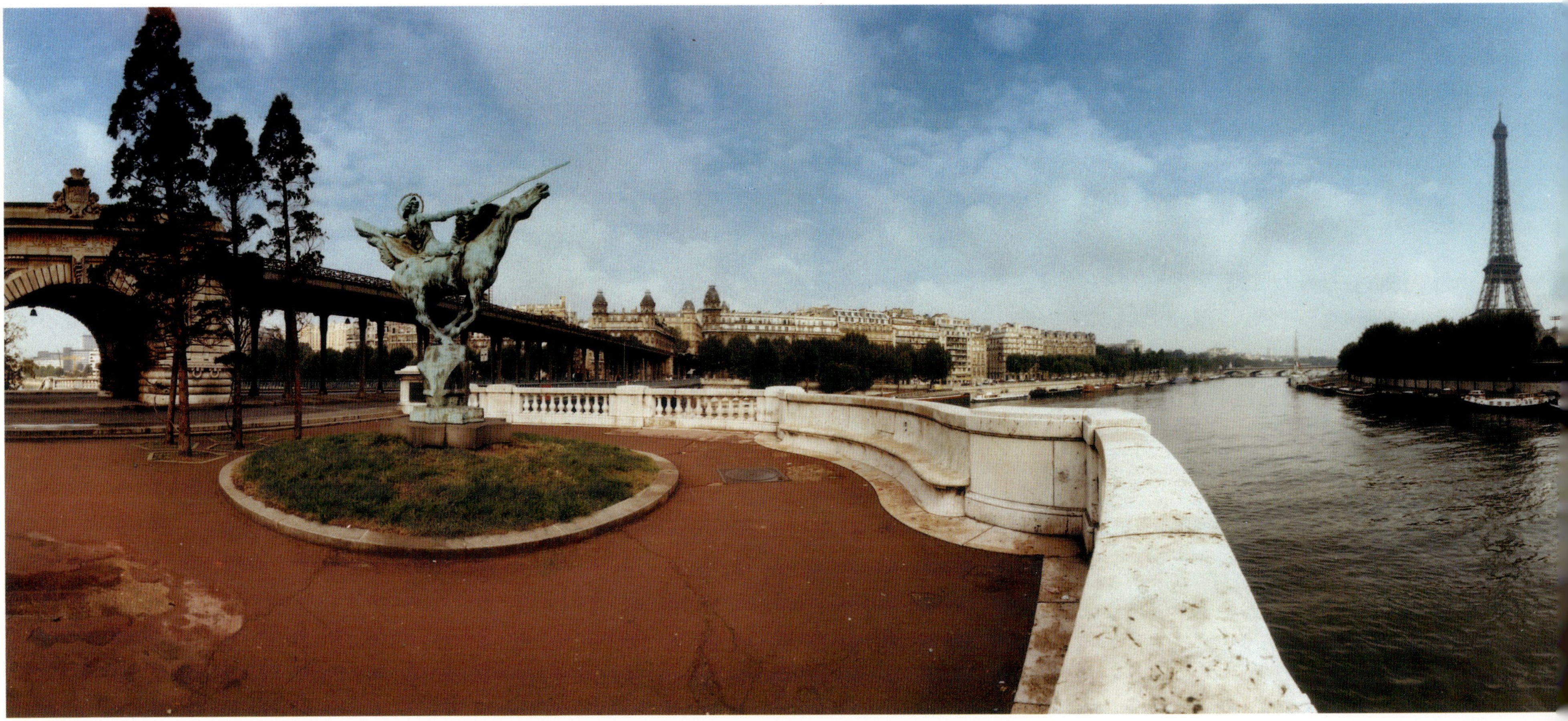

River Seine with Eiffel Tower, 1985

VENICE ROME SIENA

Piazza S. Marco, Venice, 1989

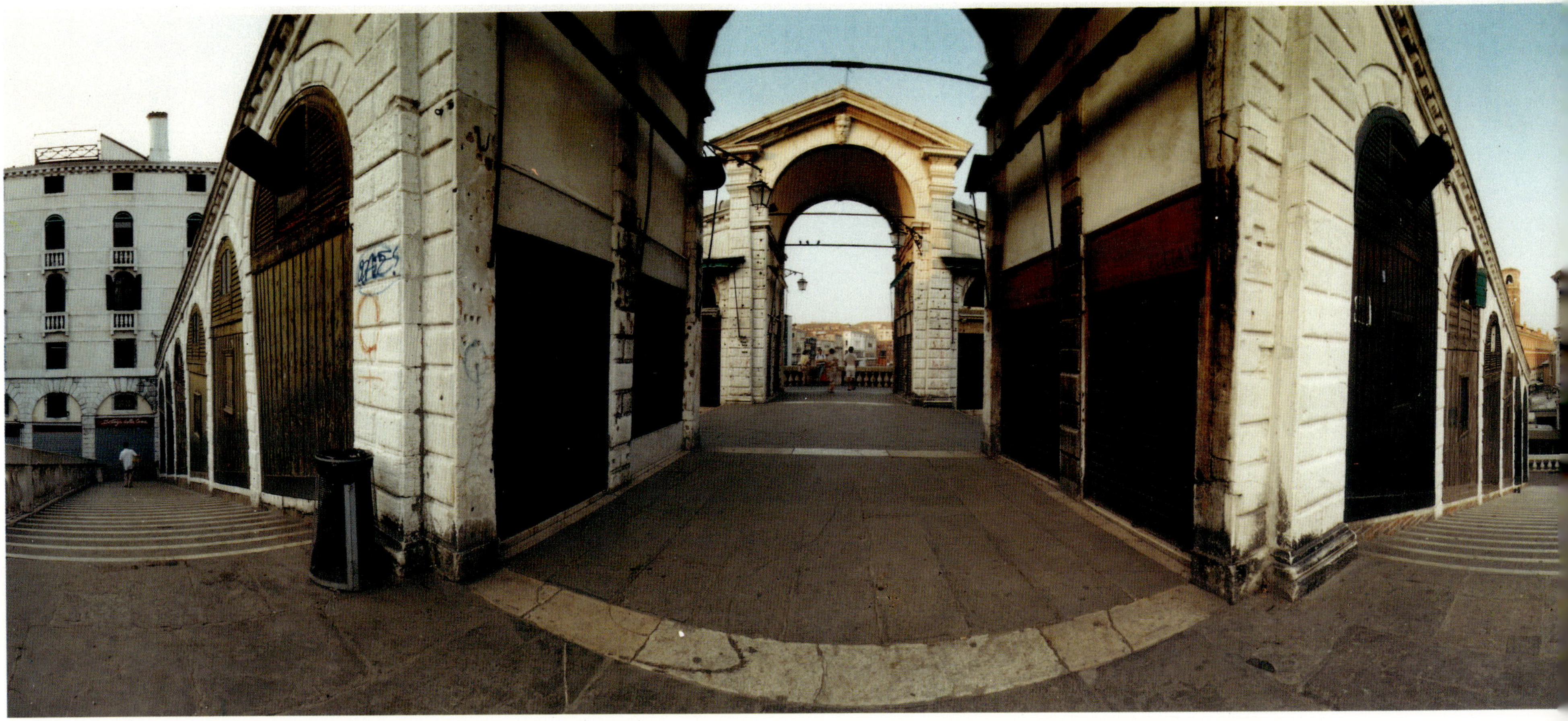

Rialto Bridge, Venice, 1989

CAMPIONATO DI SERIE A1
CARRERA
Basket
ABBONAMENTI
ESTERNONOTTE
CANALETTO
CANALETTO

Cavaletto with gondolas, Venice, 1982

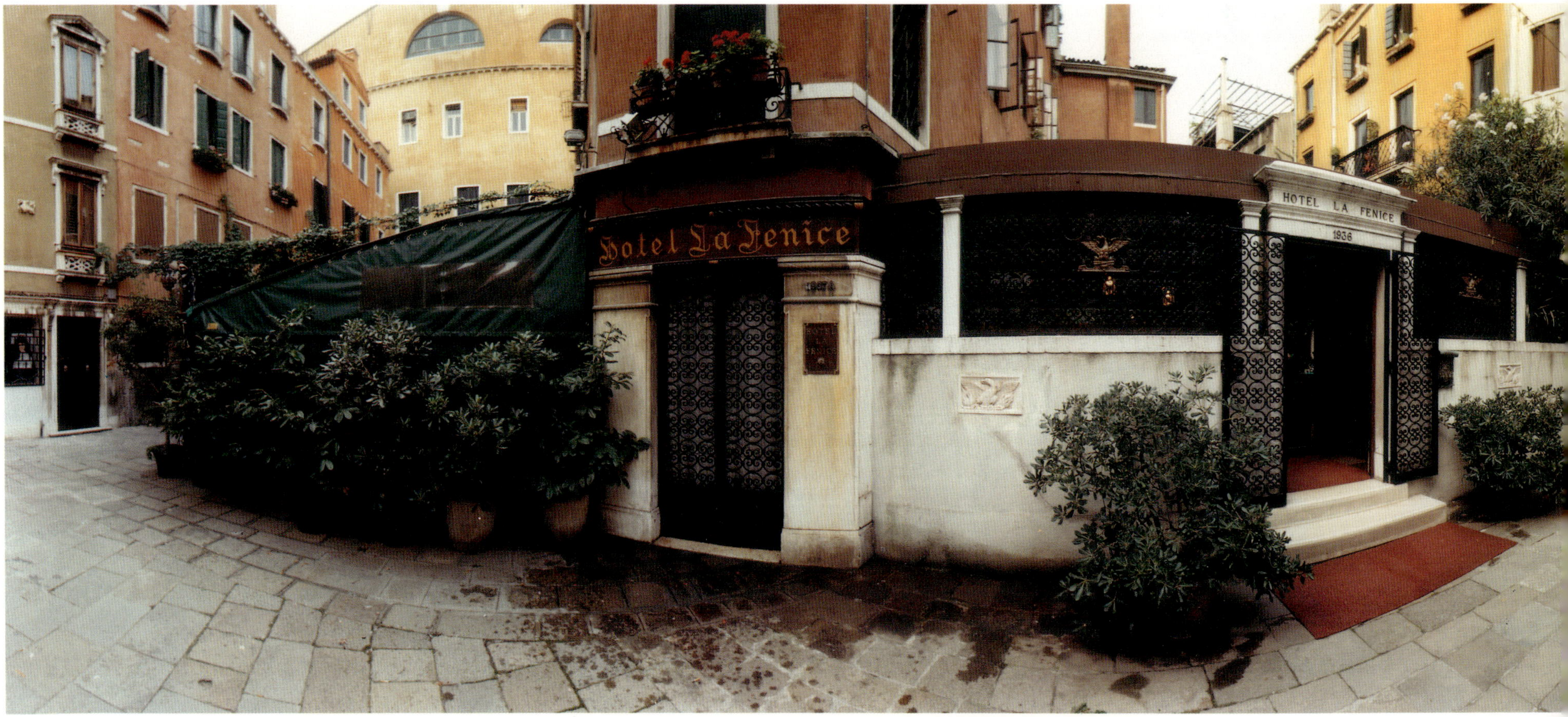
Hotel La Fenice
HOTEL LA FENICE
1936

Campiello de la Fenice, Venice, 1989

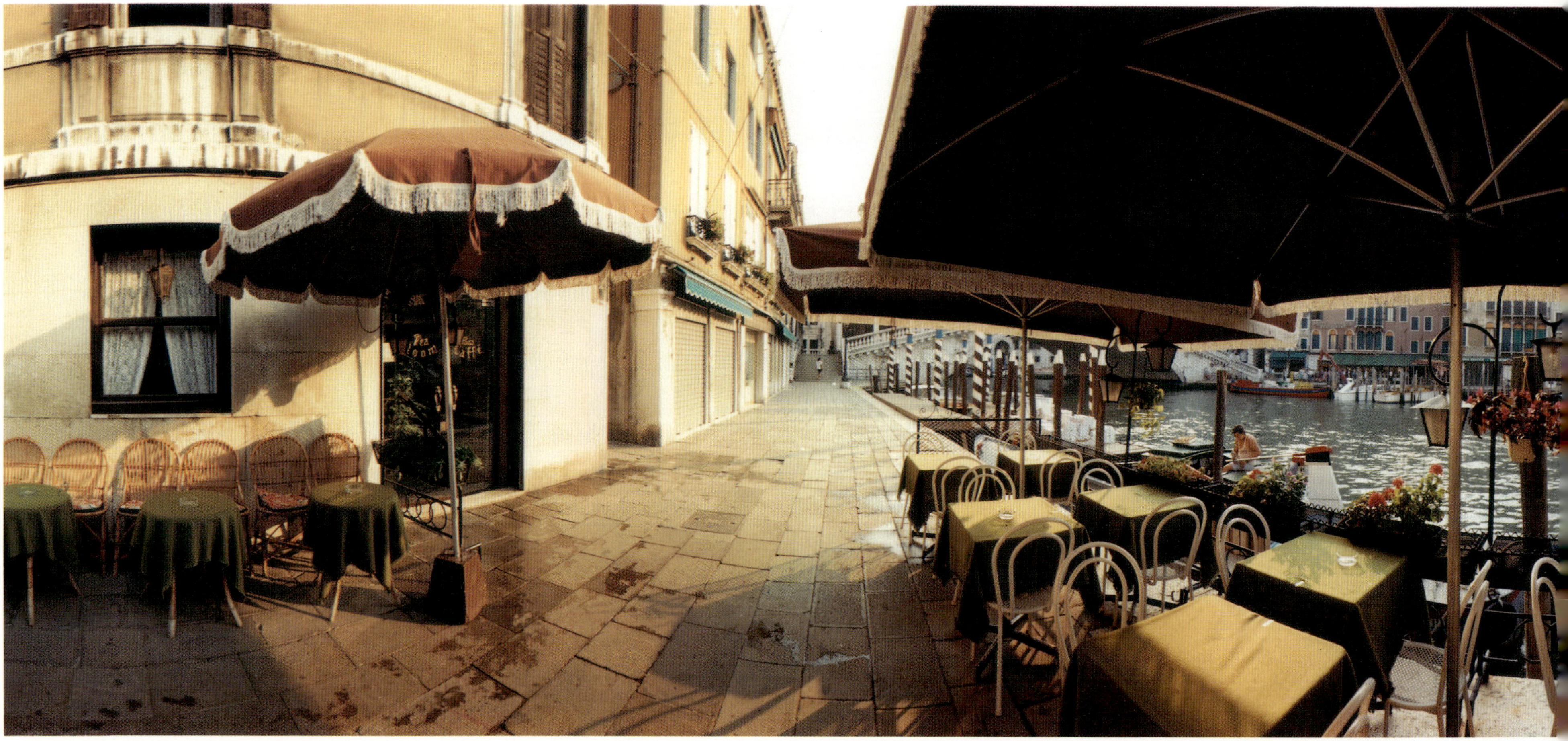

Restaurant on the Grand Canal, Venice, 1989

ECOLE DE DENTELLES
LACE SCHOOL
ESCUELA DE ENCAJES
SPITZEN SCHULE

View from Ponte del Cavaletto, Venice, 1989

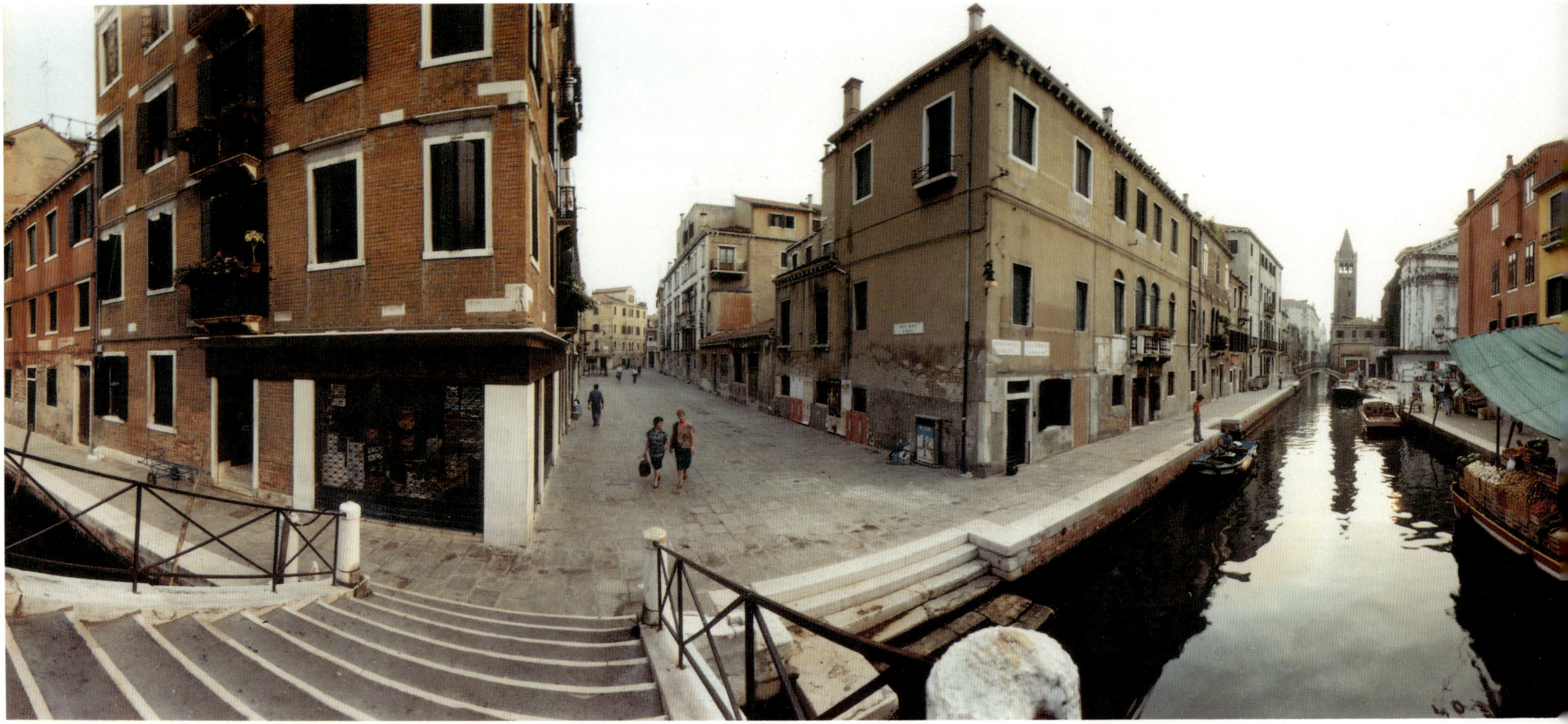

Rio de S. Barnaba, Venice, 1989

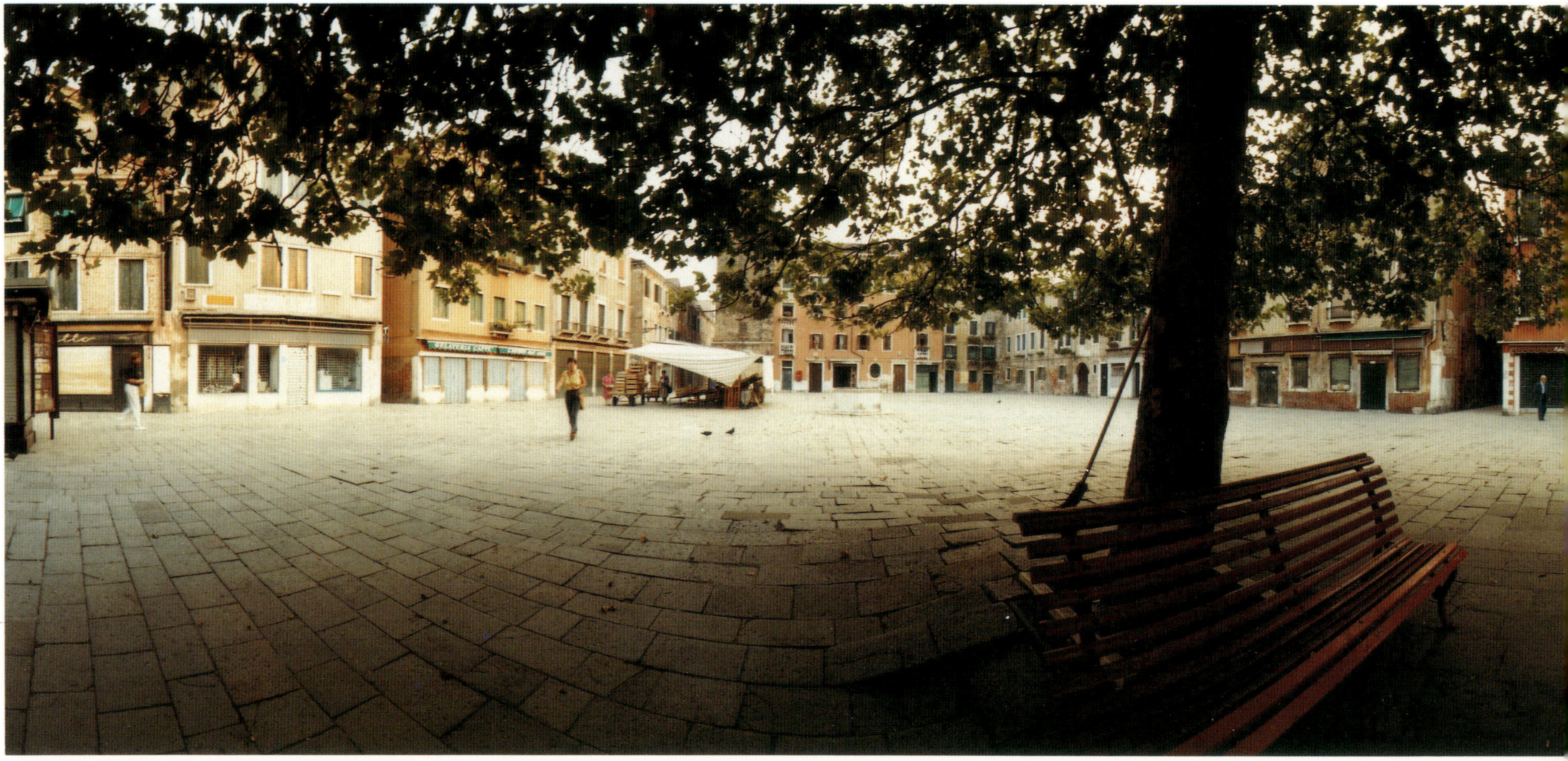

Campo S. Margherita, Venice, 1989

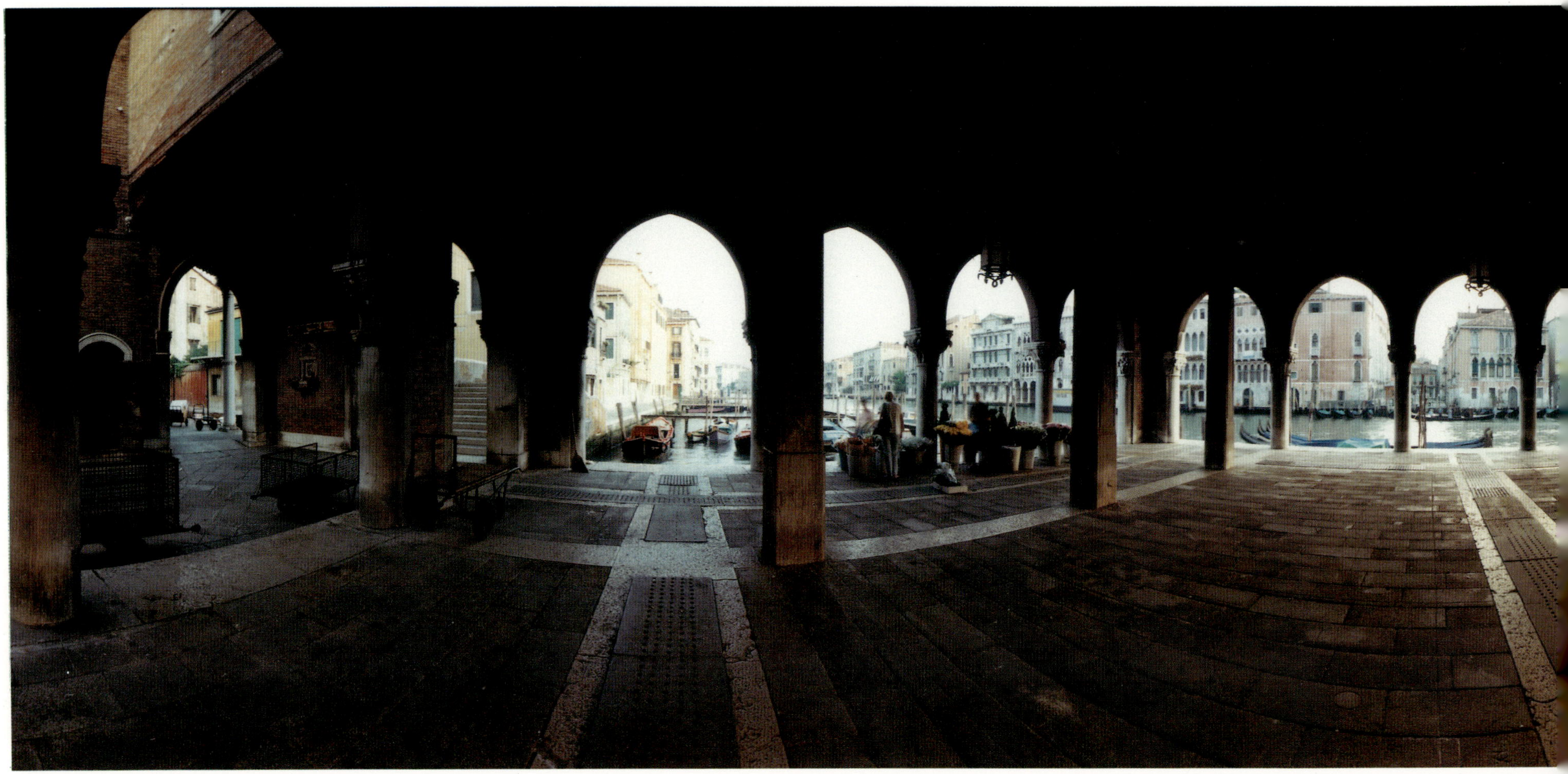

Campo Pescaria, Venice, 1989

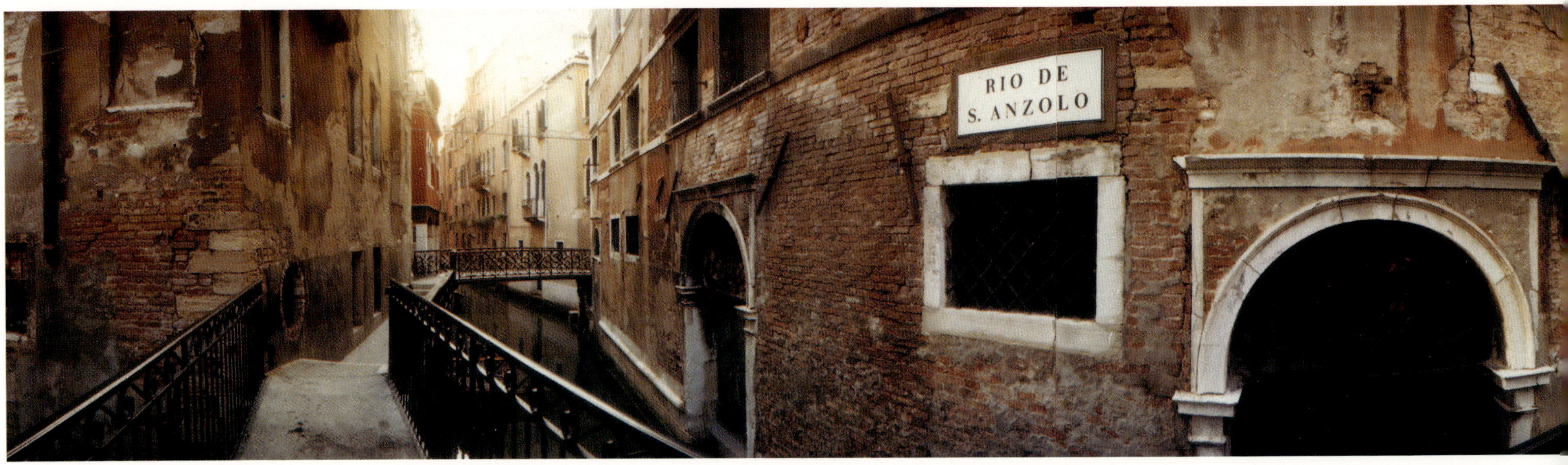
RIO DE
S. ANZOLO

Rio S. Anzolo, Venice, 1982

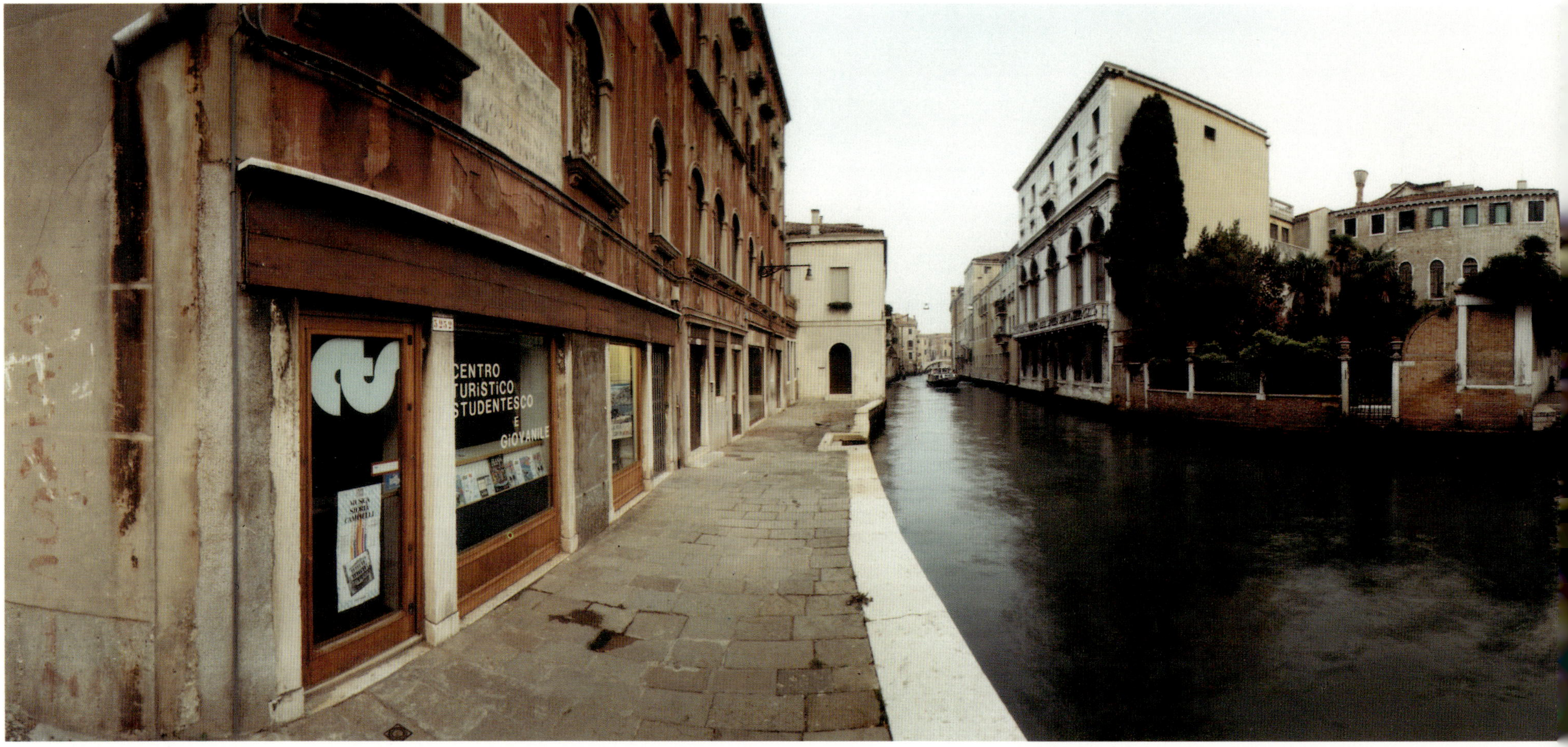
CENTRO
TURISTICO
STUDENTESCO
E
GIOVANILE

Ponte Foscari and Universita degl Studi, Venice, 1989

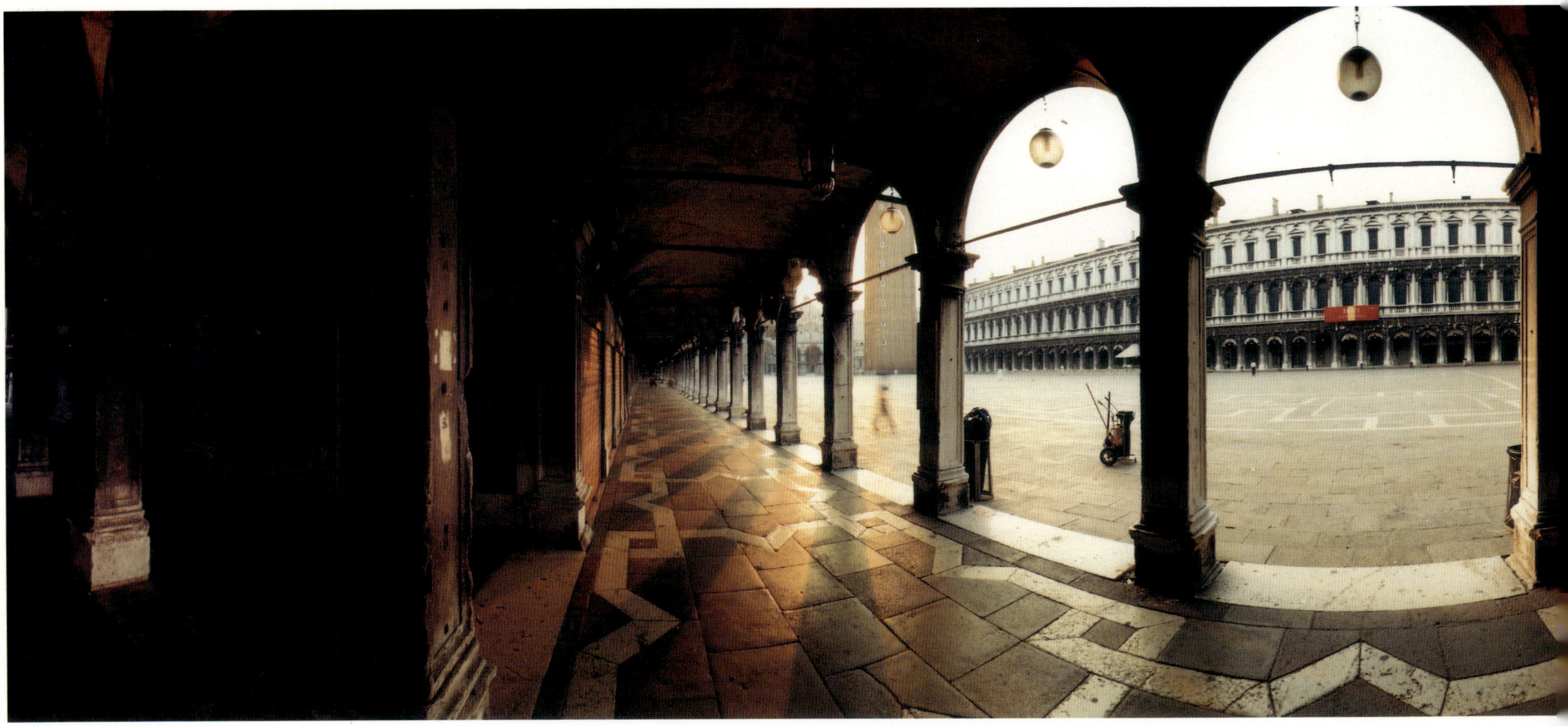

Piazza S. Marco from Procuratie Vecchie, Venice, 1989

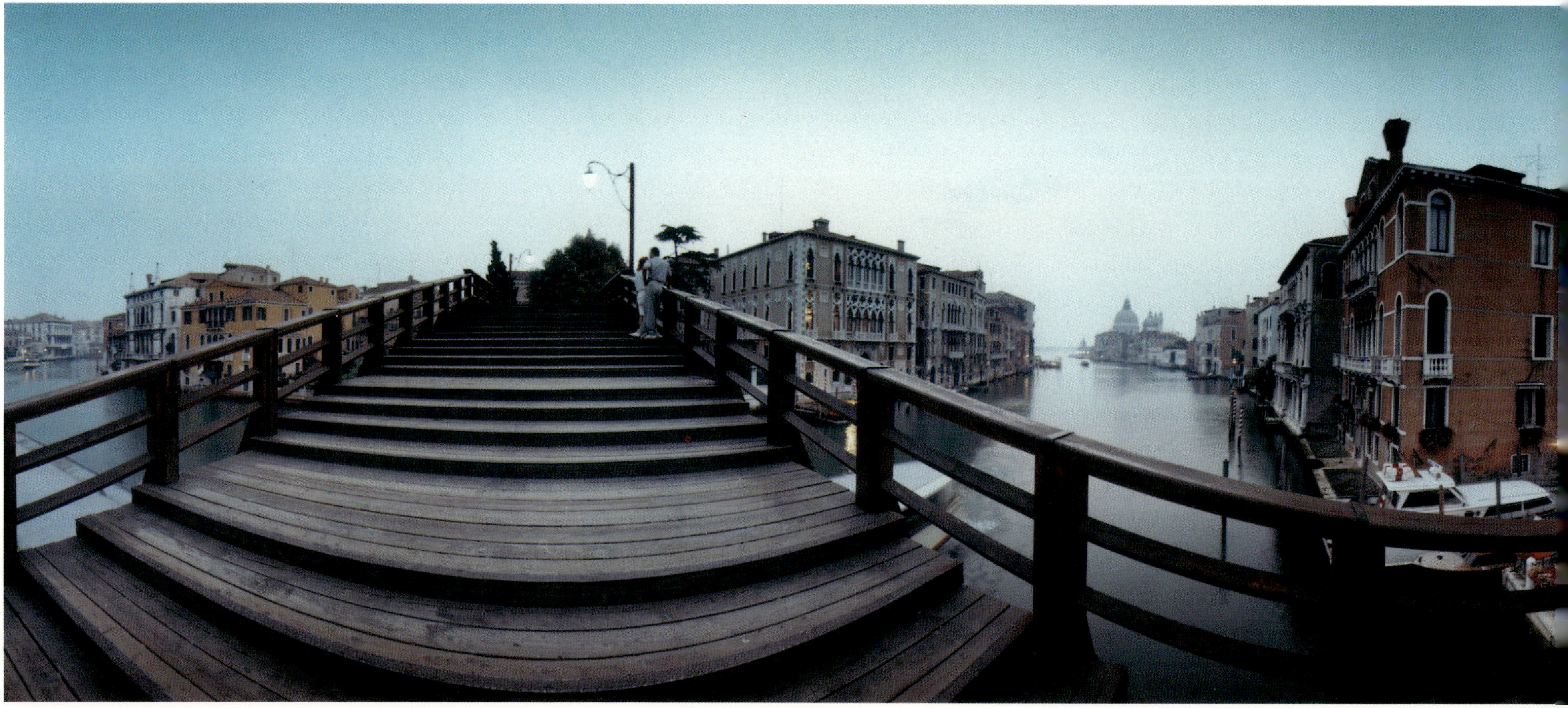

Ponte dell'Accademia, Venice, 1989

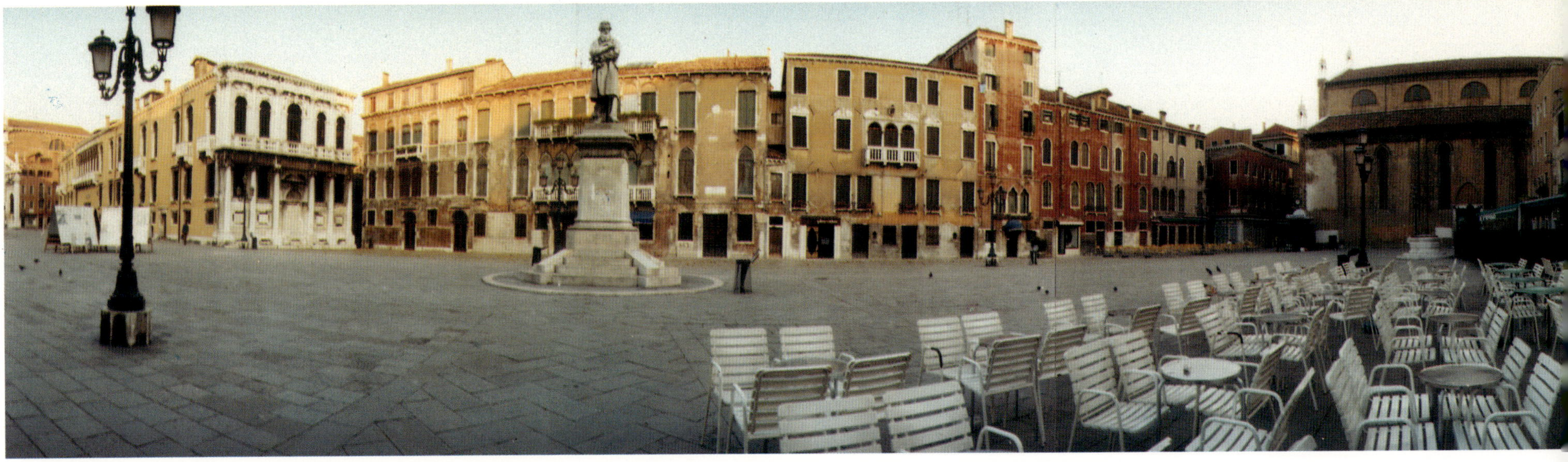

Campo Morosini, Venice, 1982

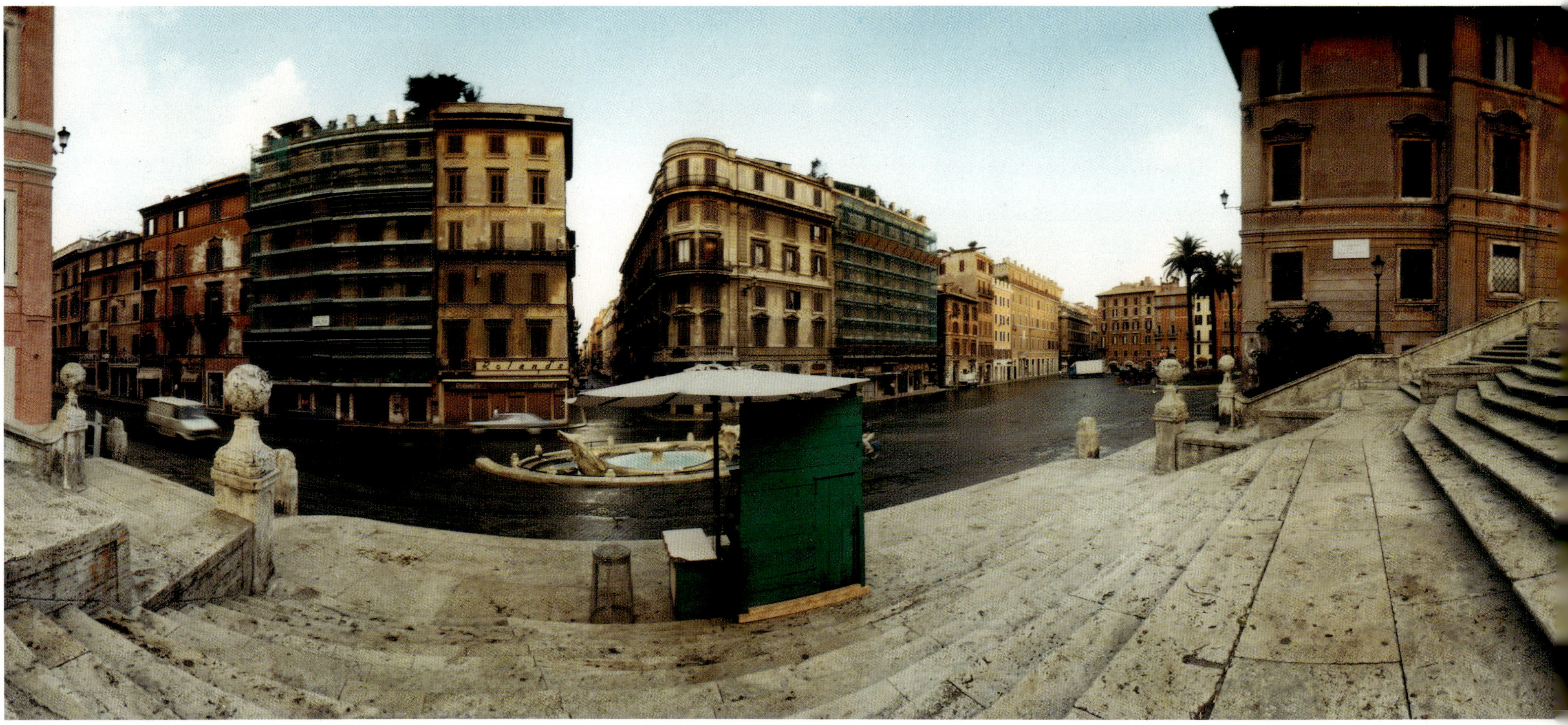

Spanish Steps, Rome, 1989

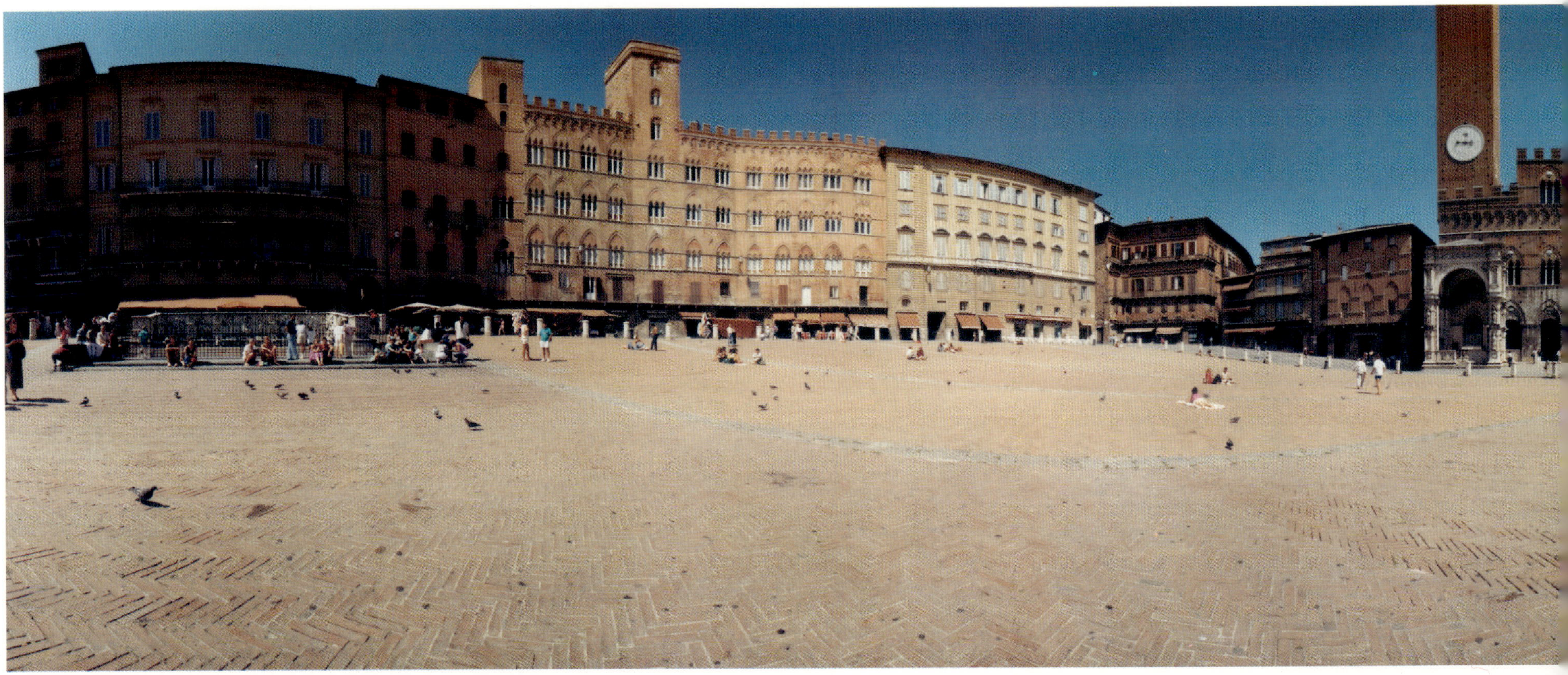

Piazza del Campo, Siena, 1989

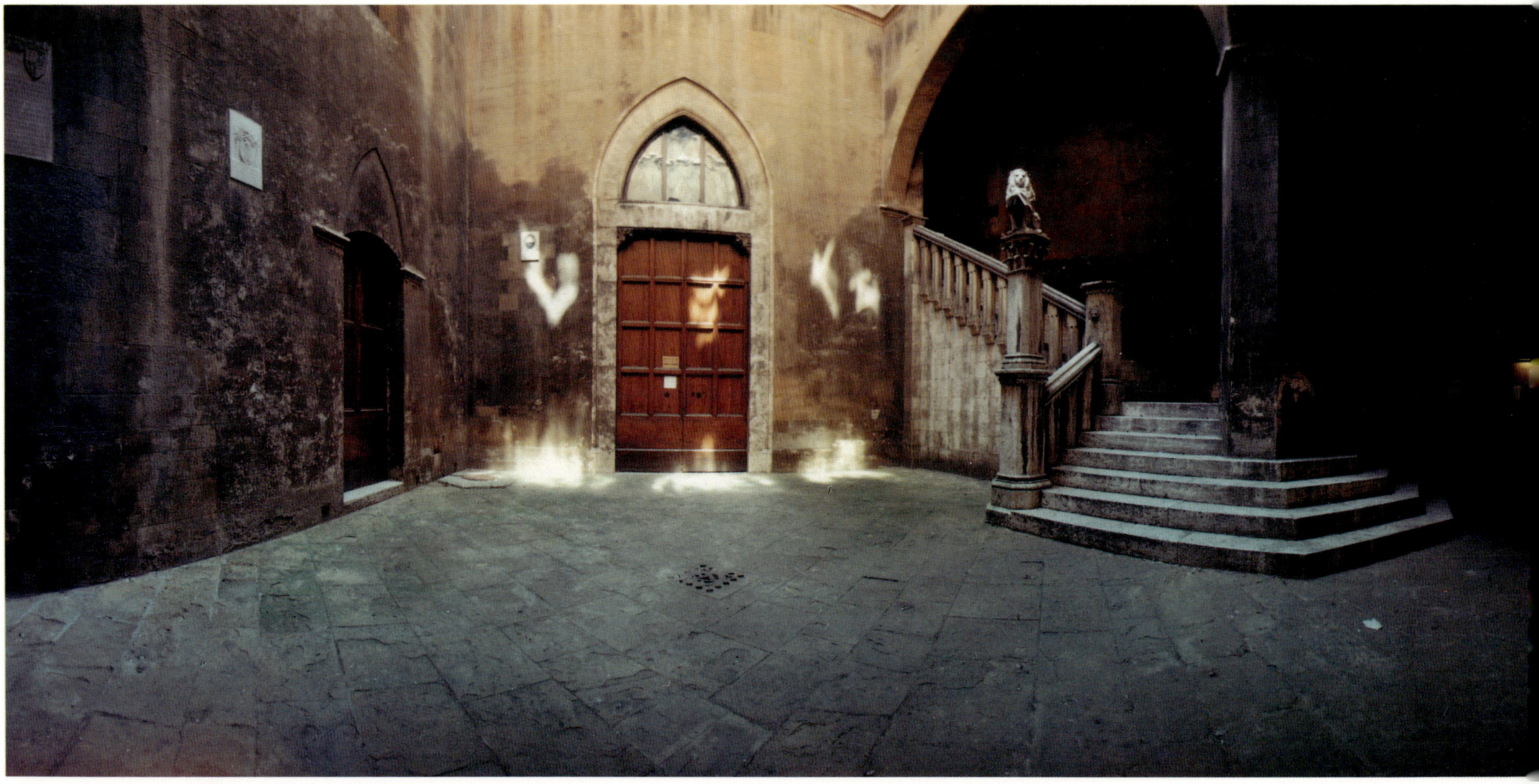

Inner court, Siena, 1989

KYOTO

Ryoan-ji Temple, Kyoto, 1989

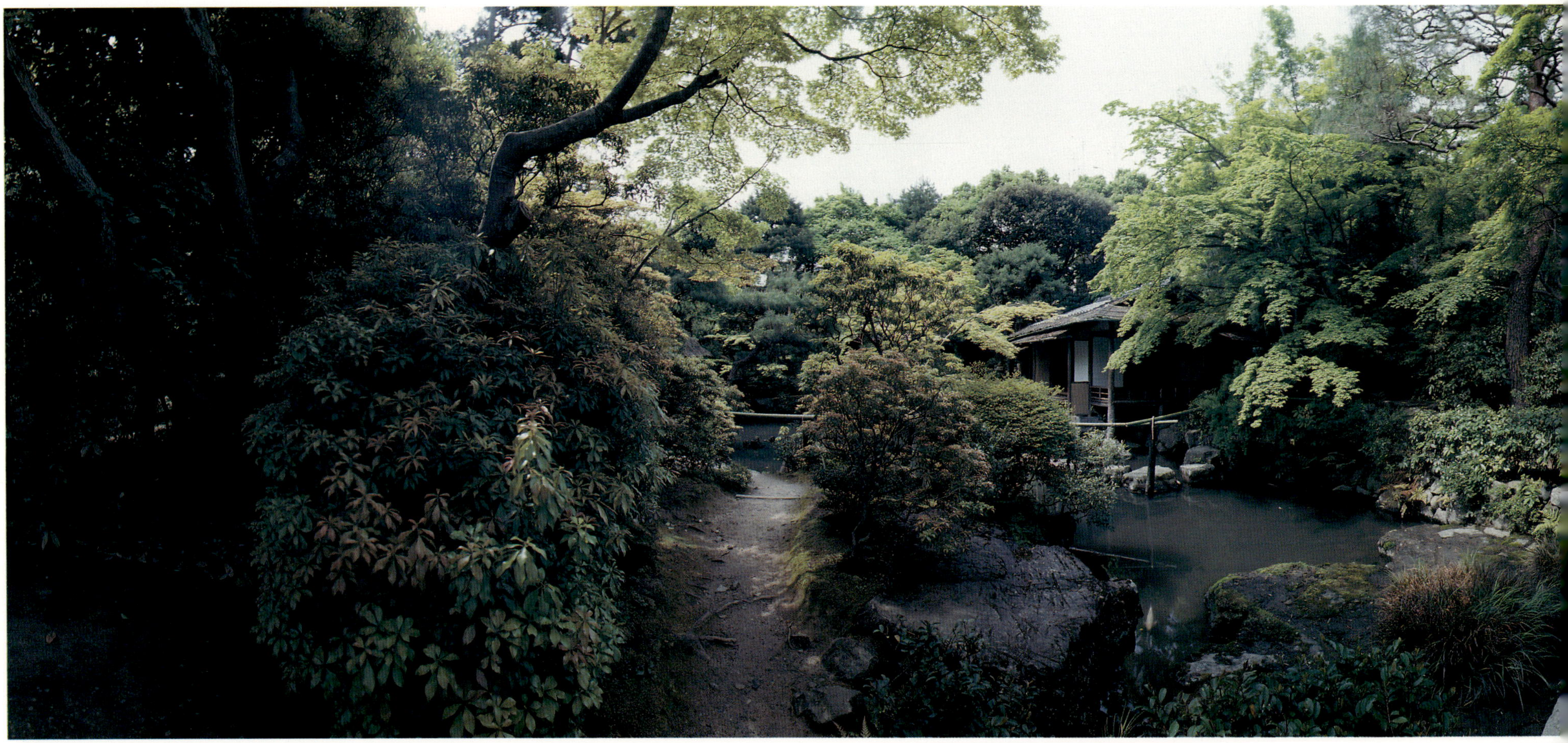

Hakusasonso Garden with pond and stone bridge, 1989

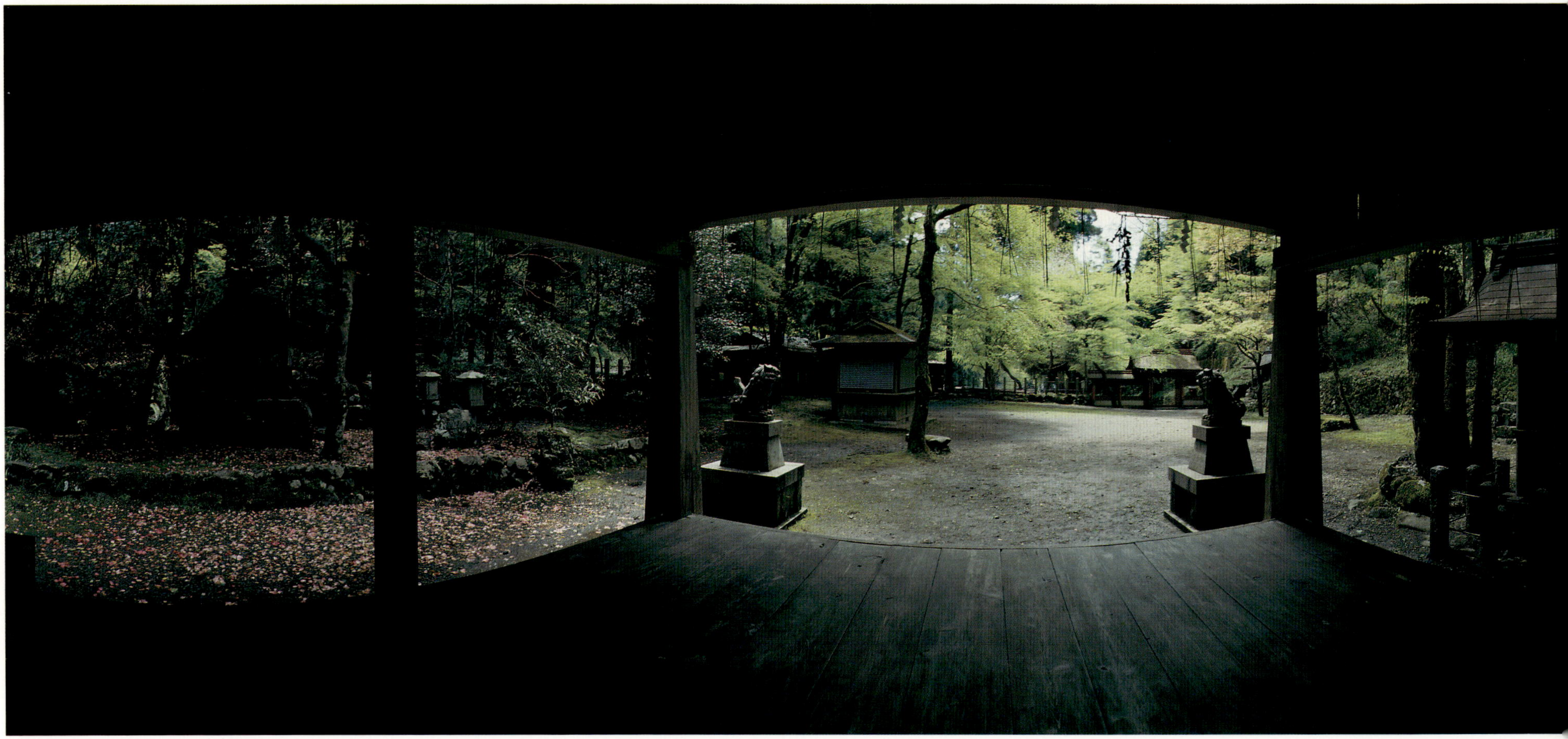

Kibune Shrine near Kyoto, 1989

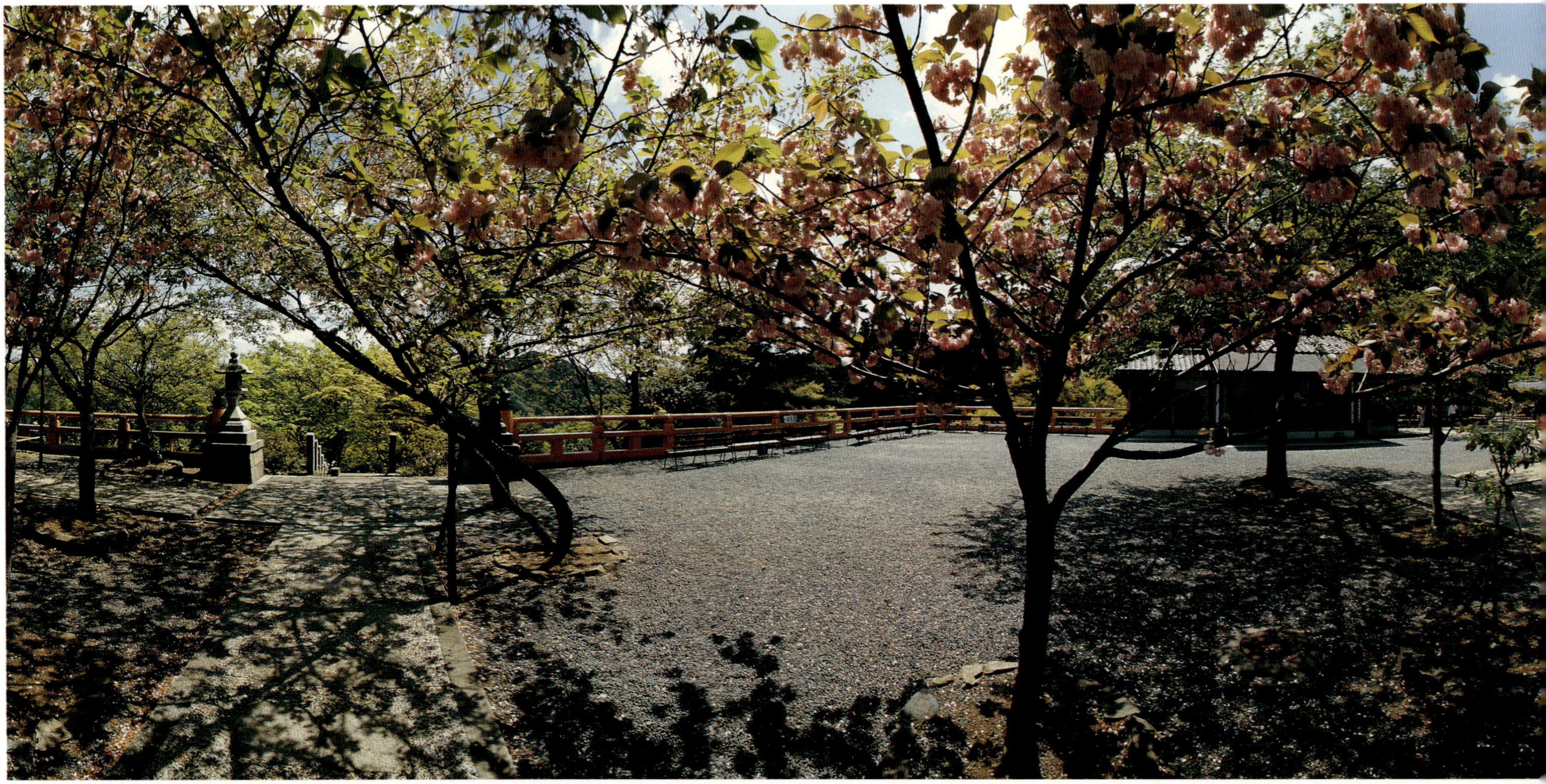

Mount Kurama, temple and cherry blossoms, 1989

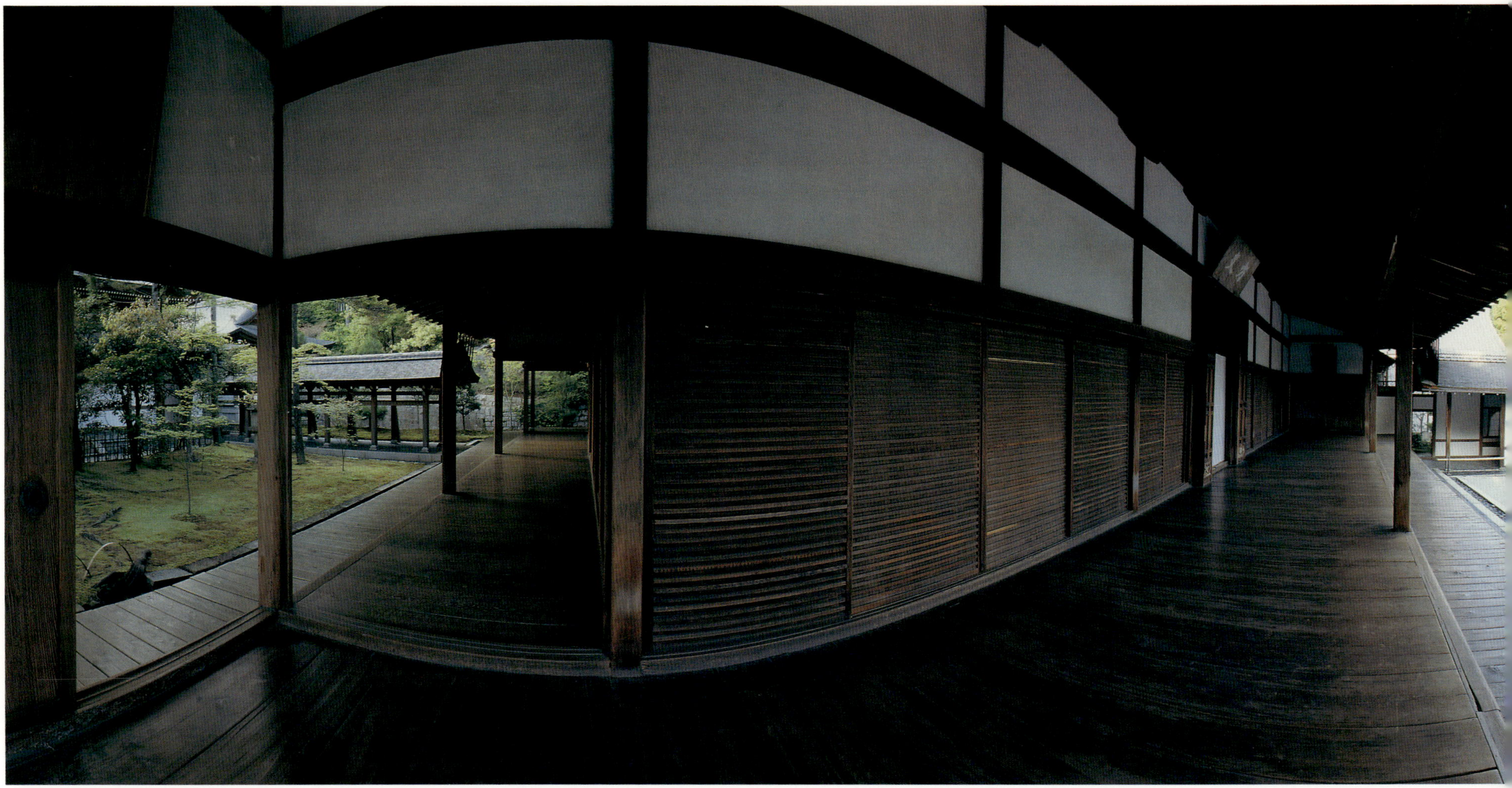

Rock garden, Ryoan-ji Temple, Kyoto, 1989

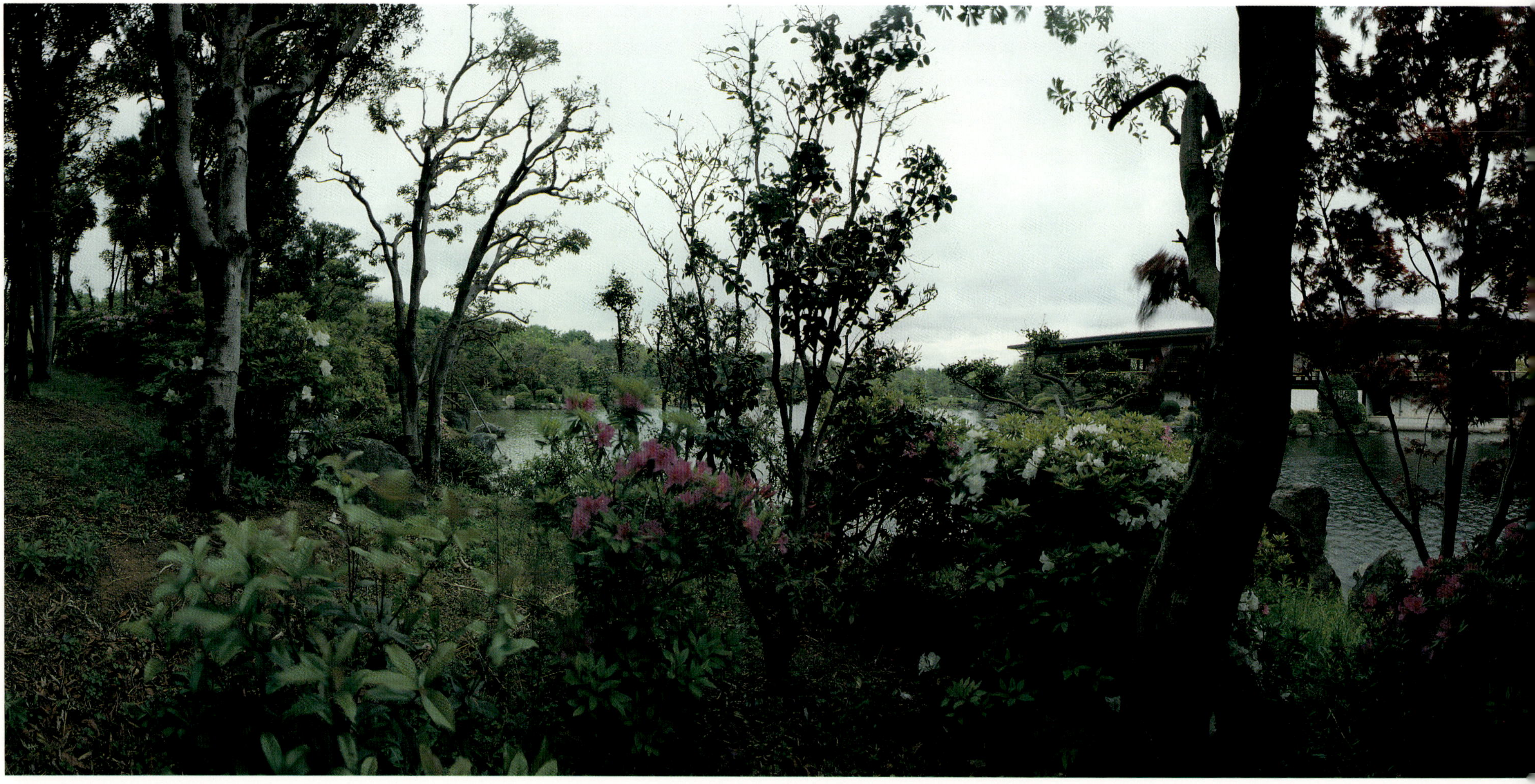

Lake Kokoro, Osaka, 1989

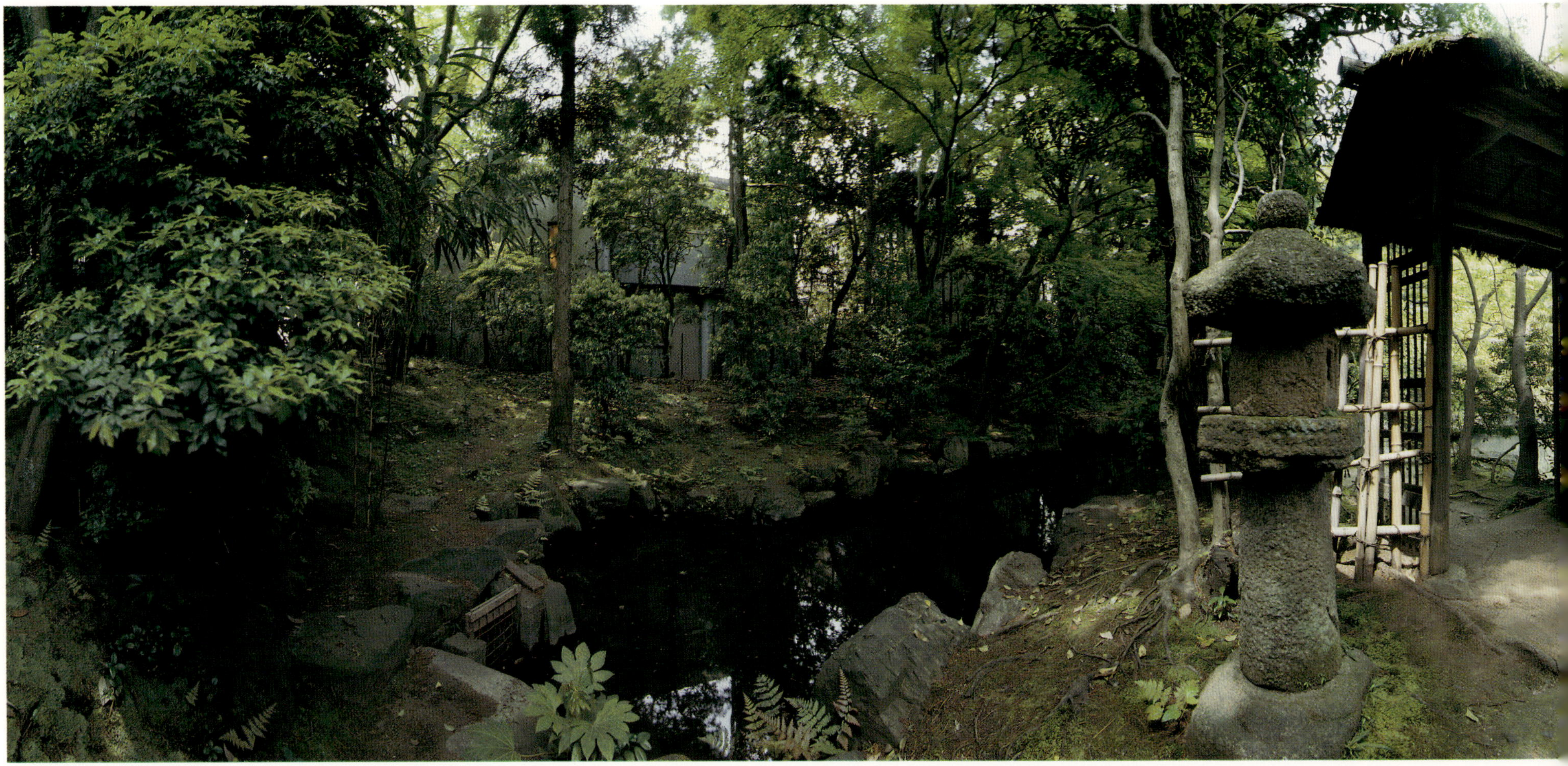

Hakusasonso Garden with stone lantern, Kyoto, 1989

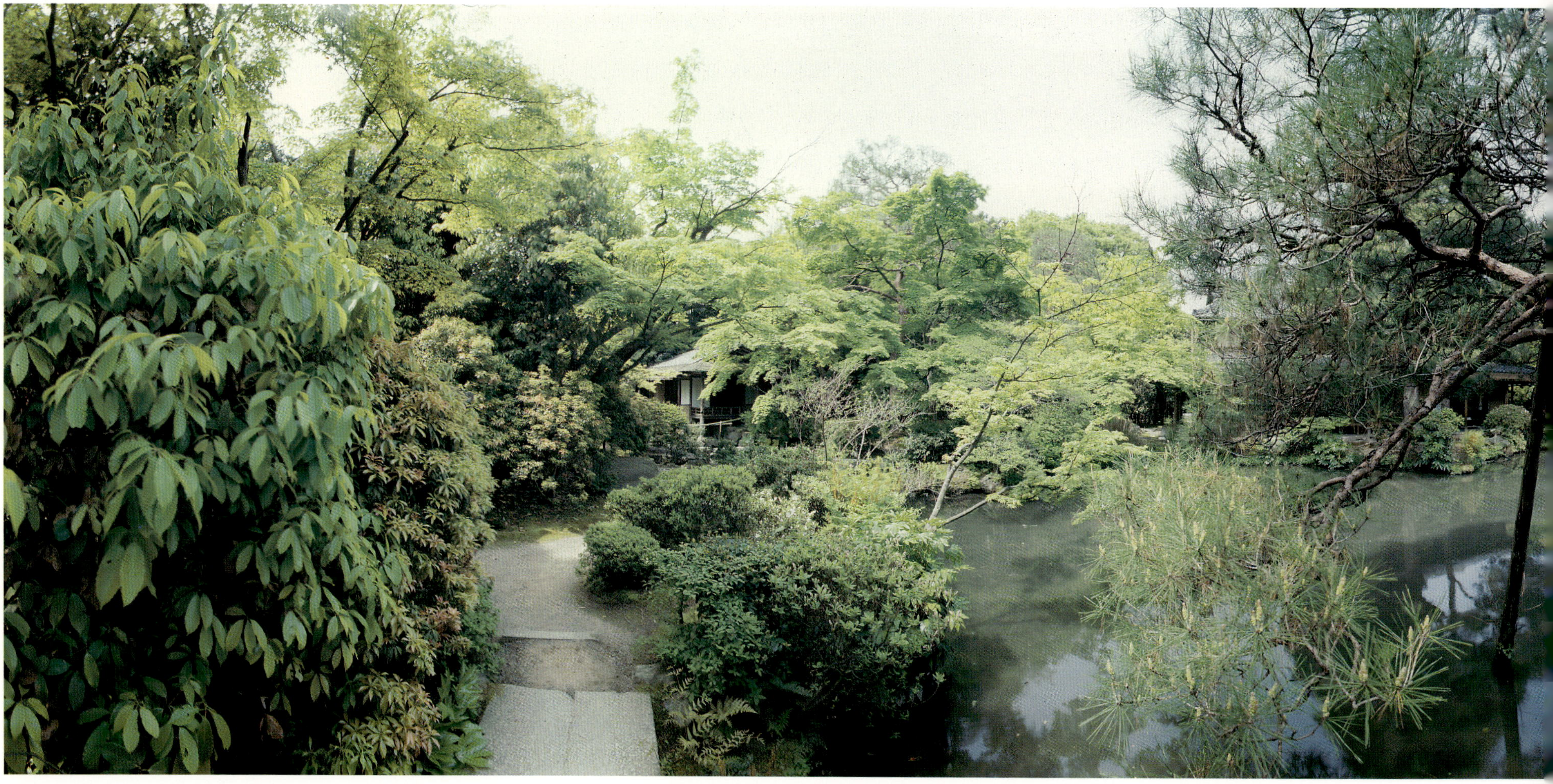

Hakusasonso Garden with blooming azalea, 1989

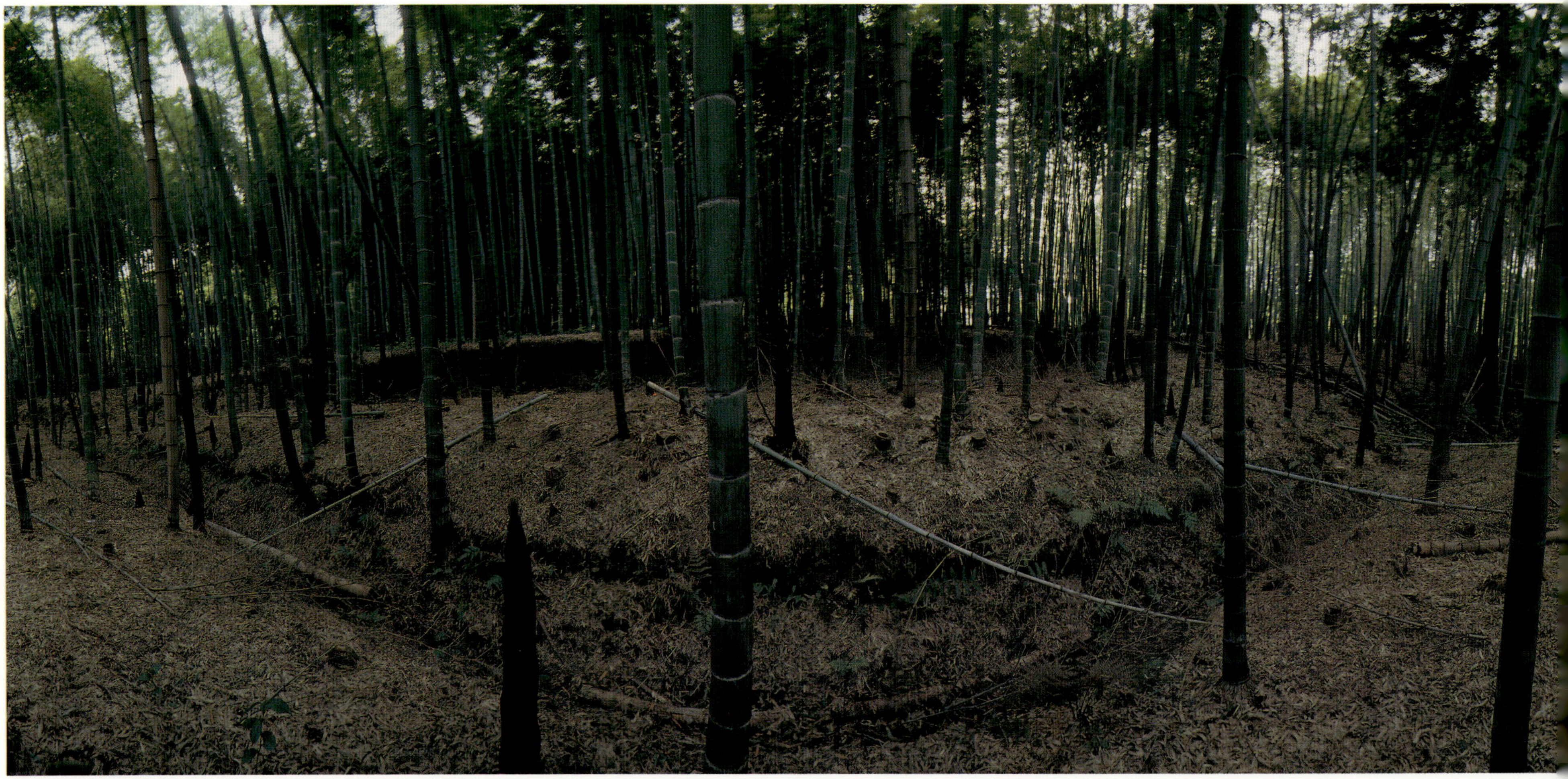

Bamboo grove, Kyoto, 1989

EVERYTHING PHOTOGRAPHIC
KENNETH SNELSON

Every photographer, in some part, is a voyeur lurking to intrude for a moment with his lens, then flee like a pirate with the prize of his latest trespass. Our curious need is to capture a piece of the world and sneak it back home.

But there are variations. I find when I'm at work with a camera I'm simply not satisfied with what is regarded as a normal window of an image. A fisheye view is okay but even a fish doesn't see what is there just behind it. My urge is to encompass the surroundings, to possess the full 360°. It's as if all the world should be included at once. It is a true voyeuristic instinct that whispers, "If you don't happen to see it here in this place, it quite likely is over there, behind the door or at the other end of the wall." All of this suggests there's a darker meaning—with its roots in some lost early experience. Though that may be, the why is often not all that interesting. I would like, though, to go into how my romance with panoramas came about.

I can pinpoint the event that triggered this panoramic passion. It was at a Berlin flea market on an afternoon in March 1975. My wife and I and our child were living in Berlin, courtesy of a D.A.A.D. fellowship. While browsing over tables piled with wonderful junk my eye came across a box camera with the label "Zeiss Ikon." Amazingly, though it was forty years old, this little jewel of a camera appeared new as if it had been sitting on a shelf all those years.

I paid a few marks for it and it was as if I had come home with a bright and shiny magic lamp. The genie emerged with memories, feelings, smells, and images of my father's camera store in the thirties. If this charming Zeiss box had survived the years so perfectly, maybe the many other cameras, sparkling in the showcase at Dad's store—Leica, Contax, Rollei, Plaubel Makina, and Voigtländer—also were still around. The nostalgia for father's camera world and the magic it had for me as a child began to fill my brain. I wanted to be close to that time and place again, to talk with my father as a grown-up. If I had the cameras of those days, it would be like finding myself in the Snelson Camera Shop once again.

The town where I grew up—Pendleton, in northeastern Oregon—is famed among rodeo followers for its Pendleton Round-up. There, my father owned the Troy Laundry and Dry Cleaners. Laundering had always been his trade, but photography was a lifelong love and cherished hobby. In 1934 when I was six—probably the worst year of the depression—Jack Snelson decided that since he and a few others in town were photo hobbyists, and since there was no real camera store, he would open one himself.

At the beginning the shop was scaled for pocketbooks of those desperate years, with a start-up stock consisting of a dozen tiny Bakelite *Norton* cameras which sold for fifty cents each—including a roll of film. But three or four years later, by the time I grew old enough to take an interest, the store had a superb line of equipment. The slogan on the letterhead read "Everything Photographic."

Around the shop I had love affairs with one camera after another and found ways to apply my young artistic talent, imitating the big name photographers in the magazines. After school and on weekends I set up tabletop miniature scenes, made montage compositions on the enlarging easel, learned how to burn in clouds (overly dramatized with deep infra red) to fill those parched, blank, eastern-Oregon skies.

One picture I made was a profound work in which I created a photographic apotheosis for a bronze equestrian statue—the only one in Pendleton—of our own hero sheriff, Tillman Taylor, killed in the line of duty decades before in a saloon shootout. Horse and rider, in my sentimental composite picture, were seen soaring skyward, hooves dissolving in a cascade of billowy clouds. I called the proud work "Til Taylor Going To Heaven."

Sometimes I tried to mimic the grotesque allegories of that curious American surrealist photographer William Mortensen. His odd spiral-bound treatise called *The Command to Look* was the only instructive material I could find on pictorial composition.

Then there were Dad's panoramic and Cirkut cameras. In those days, every town had at least one Cirkut photographer since the panoramic group-shot with all faces visible was a sure money maker. At a Shriner's or Elk's Club picnic or high school graduation, the camera could take in the entire flock. Simply by collectng a dollar-per-face, along with the list of names, a handsome day's pay was assured.

Father used his panoramic camera to capture such events as John Hamley & Company's yearly Christmas turkey presentation to its employees. I helped with the equipment and watched while Dad arranged his circle of thirty workers, each cradling a ribbon-wrapped bird. "Hold still and smile when the camera comes around," he'd instruct as the bulky box began slowly to grind its way through a revolution. Miraculously, when the picture was finished, all of Hamley's staff appeared to be placed in a perfectly straight line. Only Hamley's storefront was curved. This kind of picture taking was magical, especially when Dad took our class photo and let two or three of us scurry around back to get into the picture twice.

I left Pendleton at the end of World War II for the navy, then to study art, painting, and sculpture in college. When I came to live in New York in the early fifties, I worked in film as a cinematographer. (As a cameraman, how many movie panoramas did I shoot in those fifteen years?) I felt proud indeed of having gone so far beyond Dad's small-town camera world, yet the experience of childhood with cameras was always with me.

After our Berlin tour in 1975 I bought my first (140°, 35mm) Widelux and began to work with it, joining three panoramic frames together to simulate the complete turn of its huge cousin, the Cirkut camera. The full-circle kick was on. I next sought out the few old-timers still around to learn from them how things used to be done. I discovered the master himself, E. O. Goldbeck, in San Antonio, as well as Gabriel Allen, 90, retired, living in Florida. He had acquired all of Kodak's remaining stock of parts when they stopped producing the cameras in the forties, so I was able to buy a rare, giant, 16" model from Mr. Allen.

I completely rebuilt that big camera which, depending on the gearing and length of lens, rolls off ten or fifteen feet of film during a revolution. In order to get film I found it necessary to order a full emulsion run from Kodak in hundred-foot rolls. There was no printer around to accommodate a twelve-foot-long negative so I built my own, a long wooden box with a pressure-plate top. With its fifty or so adjustable lights it looks like nothing so much as Dracula's coffin illuminated by the Broadway Lighting Company. To make the sixty-pound outfit portable, I constructed a rack for a bicycle where I tied the camera, tripod and all. Because the lumbering machine has little capacity to stop action, I used to start out by bike each Sunday in summer at dawn when the fewest people are about and when traffic is quietest, to explore for broad expansive panoramas in the empty avenues of New York.

Finally, I found a smaller, lighter, efficient modern camera by Charles Hulcher of Hampton, Virginia. It is best designed for intimate urban places instead of the vast canyons of Manhattan, ideal to use in those worlds I love so much: the bridges, the canals, the gardens, the alleys, the small corners of Venice and Paris, as well as the temple gardens of Japan. Most of the images in this book were made with Mr. Hulcher's remarkable camera. It is a compact electronic Cirkut device which completes a rotation with nine inches of 120 film. To use this genial instrument in place of the older goliaths is age-appropriate for a photographer whose lower back is showing wear from too much lifting of large metal sculptures and ponderous panoramic cameras.

Copyright © 1990 Aperture Foundation, Inc. Photographs and "Everything Photographic" copyright © 1990 by Kenneth Snelson. "Music Box" copyright © 1990 by Laurance Wieder. All rights reserved under International and Pan-American Copyright Conventions. Composed by David E. Seham Associates, Inc., Metuchen, New Jersey. Printed and bound in Hong Kong by South China Printing Company (1988) Ltd.

Library of Congress Catalog Number 90-081489
ISBN 0-89381-438-5 hardcover

The staff at Aperture for *Full Circle* is Michael E. Hoffman, Executive Director; Steve Dietz, Editor; Jane D. Marsching, Assistant Editor; Stevan Baron, Production Director; Linda Tarrack, Production Associate. Book design by Wendy Byrne.

Aperture Foundation, Inc., publishes a periodical, books, and portfolios of fine photography to communicate with serious photographers and creative people everywhere. A complete catalog is available upon request. Address: 20 East 23 Street, New York, NY 10010.